THE BOOK OF MICHAEL

SEVENFOLD DOCTRINE

BY

MICHAEL HARRIS

PROJECT PRIME MARKETING

Documenting the ship at Temple Mount in 2011 and the UFO from Winnipeg, Manitoba 1971 I believe. Both did a double flash before they vanished. Possible communication. The flash goes back to before the time of Christ and Christ. The Form of the Star it's called in the books or star, or great light meaning big light.

Sevenfold Doctrine

The seven thunders are the elements and time for seven millennium being stuck together to change weather raise the dead alter all things on earth. Being seven time more, or seven time stronger.

That angels out of the east is being resurrected from the earth, this happens after the resurrection.

Secrets of Enoch 40
6 And I investigated all things, and wrote the road of the thunder and of the lightning, and they showed me the keys and their guardians, their rise, the way they go; it is let out in measure (sc. gently) by a chain, lest by a heavy chain and violence it hurl down the angry clouds and destroy all things on earth.

"And after these things I saw four angels standing on the four corners of the earth, holding the four winds of the earth, that the wind should not blow on the earth, nor on the sea, nor on any tree. And I saw another angel ascending from the east, having the seal of the living God: and he cried with a loud voice to the four angels, to whom it was given to hurt the earth and the sea, saying, Hurt not the earth, neither the sea, nor the trees, till we have sealed the servants of our God in their foreheads."
Revelation 7:1-3 KJV

"And when the seven thunders had uttered their voices, I was about to write: and I heard a voice from heaven saying unto me, Seal up those things which the seven thunders uttered, and write them not."
Revelation 10:4 KJV

"Moreover the light of the moon shall be as the light of the sun, and the light of the sun shall be sevenfold, as the light of seven days, in the day that the LORD bindeth up the breach of his people, and healeth the stroke of their wound."
Isaiah 30:26 KJV

"Thus saith the LORD of hosts, Behold, evil shall go forth from nation to nation, and a great whirlwind shall be raised up from the coasts of the earth. And the slain of the LORD shall be at that day from one end of the earth even unto the other end of the earth: they shall not be lamented, neither gathered, nor buried; they shall be dung upon the ground."
Jeremiah 25:32-33 KJV

"For a fire is kindled in mine anger, and shall burn unto the lowest hell, and shall consume the earth with her increase, and set on fire the foundations of the mountains."
Deuteronomy 32:22 KJV

in·crease
verb
/inˈkrēs/
become or make greater in size, amount, intensity, or degree.

Letters of Herod and Pilot
Now when he was crucified, there was darkness over all the world, and the sun was obscured for half a day, and the stars appeared, but no lustre was seen in them; and the moon lost its brightness, as though tinged with blood;

And at the third hour of the night the sun appeared more luminous than it had ever shone, lighting up the whole hemisphere. And as lightning-flashes suddenly come forth in a storm,

And the heaven became seven times more luminous than on all other days. And at the third hour of the night the sun appeared more luminous than it had ever shone, lighting up the whole hemisphere. And as lightning-flashes suddenly come forth in a storm,

And on the first day of the week, about the third hour of the night, the sun appeared as it never shone before, and the whole heaven became bright. And as lightnings come in a storm,

And amid the terror dead men were seen rising again, so that the Jews who saw it said, We beheld Abraham and Isaac, and Jacob, and the twelve patriarchs, who died some two thousand five hundred years before, and we beheld Noah clearly in the body. And all the multitude walked about and sang hymns to God with a loud voice, saying, The Lord our God, who hath risen from the dead, hath made alive all the dead,

Esdras 15:
38 And then shall there come great storms from the south, and from the north, and another part from the west.
39 And strong winds shall arise from the east, and shall open it; and the cloud which he raised up in wrath, and the star stirred to cause fear toward the east and west wind, shall be destroyed.
40 The great and mighty clouds shall be puffed up full of wrath, and the star, that they may make all the earth afraid, and them that dwell therein; and they shall pour out over every high and eminent place a horrible star,
41 Fire, and hail, and flying swords, and many waters, that all fields may be full, and all rivers, with the abundance of great waters.
42 And they shall break down the cities and walls, mountains and hills, trees of the wood, and grass of the meadows, and their corn.

Herod and Pilot
And as lightnings come in a storm, so certain men of lofty stature, in beautiful array, and of indescribable glory, appeared in the air, and a countless host of angels,

This is the stuff of prophecy.

Science
What would happen if Earth had 10x more oxygen?
In the event of doubling the oxygen levels on Earth, the most significant changes would be the speeding up of processes like respiration and combustion. With the presence of more fuel, i.e. oxygen, forest fires would become more massive and devastating. Wet vegetation would not provide protection either.

Let me explain, my interpretation.

Quizlet?

Carbon dioxide increases in the atmosphere, this affects global temperature which in turn affects the initial disturbance of carbon dioxide. (Carbon dioxide increases, causing temperatures to increase, causing CO_2 to be released from the oceans which will cause CO_2 to rise in the atmosphere.

What force pushes the plates apart?
Heat and gravity are fundamental to the process.

Lithospheric plates are part of a planetary scale thermal convection system. The energy source for plate tectonics is Earth's internal heat while the forces moving the plates are the "ridge push" and "slab pull" gravity forces.

Among those souls, yet are not yet born, and the resurrection at the end, when time gets stuck together. The books say Time is Stuck together, which give those in the future the ability to come back to us.

So, if there is any evidence as to the heavens being created in a period time that is stuck together? Saying if things are sped up and atmospheres combined for seven millennium. That the atmosphere would be changed and become stronger and more violent.

"And after these things I saw four angels standing on the four corners of the earth, holding the four winds of the earth, that the wind should not blow on the earth, nor on the sea, nor on any tree. And I saw another angel ascending from the east, having the seal of the living God: and he cried with a loud voice to the four angels, to whom it was given to hurt the earth and the sea,"
Revelation 7:1-2 KJV

Copyright © 2023 Michael Harris.

All rights reserved.

No part of this publication may be reproduced, distributed, or transmitted in any form or by any means, including photocopying, recording, or other electronic or mechanical methods without the prior written permission of the publisher, except in the case of brief quotations embodied in critical reviews and certain other noncommercial uses permitted by copyright law. For permission requests, write to the author at:

Copyright © Registration No.: TXu002360004

Technical House Games & Entertainment
Michael Dennis Harris
13625 Lyndon B Johnson St
Manor, TX 78653 United States

ISBN: (eBook): 9781088129104
ISBN: (Paperback): 9781088129074
ISBN: (Hardcover): 9781088129272

Front cover image by Project Prime Marketing.
Book design by Project Prime Marketing.

First printing edition 2023.

Project Prime Marketing
www.projectprimemktg.com

DEDICATION

I would like to thank Project Prime Marketing, for developing a system to assist writers to succeed in the field of writing and entertainment.

Second this is dedicated to people who think they know your thoughts, yet you are incapable of doing what you practice. So, many are wrongly judged by all you imagine.

This is a dedication to two or three prophets, apostles and witnesses being made credible again in the teaching of the word of God.

That Christian Law is Certified as being more credible than Canon Law which I seek to overthrow by its limitations. Which are not limitations made by God or men of God, but men. Dedicated to the teaching of Telepathy which, if we teach one teaching to all men of earth. If that teaching is good, it makes all men of earth equal as a standard of Telepathy. It's required to be equal to see Telepathy by design. And again special thanks to project prime marketing for this opportunity to express something close to my heart.

EPIGRAPH

The Story of Christ is a story of a man who jumped so far back in time, nothing existed. He left Heaven as a sign to prove he was here. Like Kilroy was here so to speak.
Colossians 1:17 their telling you Christ jumped back in time before all things.
"And he is before all things, and by him all things consist."
Colossians 1:17 KJV

Question: Time Travel is or Time Stuck together the only way a man born on earth could go back before all things. Further those clothed in white happen maybe after judgement and judgments does not happen till the throne built. The Throne may not be built for 1500 years, and judgments after that.

be·fore
/bəˈfôr/
adverb
during the period of time preceding a particular event or time.

"All things were made by him; and without him was not anything made that was made."
John 1:3 KJV

Deductive Reasoning says, because of that statement in John 1:3 the planet Christ came from vanished from existence while traveling back in Time, because he's before all things. The Solution to the problems God left us is Time, being stopped or failing, which solution also for raising the dead.

"And to make all men see what is the fellowship of the mystery, which from the beginning of the world hath been hid in God, who created all things by Jesus Christ:"
Ephesians 3:9 KJV

Time Travel back in time would cause all things to vanish, Deductive Reasoning says because time failed, they could be from a million years in the future. So, raising the dead is possible.

TABLE OF CONTENTS

Foreword	01
Preface	04
Dedication	10
Introduction	11
Prologue	13
Epigraph	17
Eyes opened	18
Chapter 1 EYES OPENED / POSSIBLE	25
Eyes opened	25
Possible Contact	25
Eighth Day and Time Travel explanations	28
Chapter 2 TIME STUCK TOGETHER	32
Time Stuck Together	32
Effects on Plants	32
Time Stuck Together to cause the flood.	33
Time Stuck Together to Raise the Dead	34
Christ and Michael Question	38
Aeon and Time Travel parts	38
Chapter 3 KINGDOM OF GOD CAME, BUT BOOKS REMOVE	46
Evidence of Time Stuck Together	46
Effects of Time Stuck Together	49
Chapter 4 TIME TRAVEL & ANGELS	52
Eighth Day / Time Travel	52
Those Sent to Teach from The 1000 Year Period	53
Supposition of Michael	57

Judah Claimed to Be an Angel	59
The Six Men Are Archangels When Raise from the Dead	60
Who is He Who Readeth	62

Chapter 5 SUPPOSITION OF CHRIST — 73

Evidence of Zero Time	74
These Are Thought Related Issues Related to foreign thought	83

Chapter 6 REBORN — 87

Possibility these children may have been reinserted or reborn again	87

Chapter 7 TELEPATHIC CHILDREN — 93

Chapter 8 CHRISTIAN LAW / TELEPATHY — 100

The Kingdom of Heaven	100
Sevenfold Doctrine of The Whole Creation	100
The True Doctrine Based on Two or Three	100
Concepts of Telepathy	101
Study of Telepathy	103

Chapter 9 THRONE — 122

Evidence Time Stopped	127
Form of The Star	128

Chapter 10 SOME RESURRECTED WERE PERHAPS NOT YET BORN — 134

Time Stuck Together	134

Chapter 11 CREATION / SCIENCE — 143

Chapter 12 THE WAR IN HEAVEN — 158

Prophecy	162

Moneyless System	162
Towards The End of the 1000 Years Of Resurrection	163
Some Angelic Evil Resurrection	163
Satan and the Fallen angels Time Jump	163
Fallen angels Jump Back in Time	164
Time Travel	164
Note Satan Is Black	164
Monetary System is reestablished	165
Causing The Battle of Armageddon	165
Question of the seventy angels	166
Revelation 12 the War in Heaven	166
Time Travel Back in Time Crime	175
The Teachings of Michael	179
But what we don't see is the moneyless system being taught	181
Those sent to teach in the thousand-year period.	183
These Are Those Who Reestablished the Monetary System`	186
The true teaching is founded on two or three.	189

Chapter 13 RESURRECTION — 195

Moneyless System is Established	196
These Are Those Who Reestablished the monetary system.	199
The True Teaching is Founded on Two or Three	204
Fell before their time arrived = time travel crime	217

AFTERWORDS	223
CONCLUSION	224
CHRONOLOGY	231
GLOSSARY	232
BIBLIOGRAPHY	246
AUTOBIOGRAPHY	249

FOREWORD

"Lost time is never found again" a famous quote by Benjamin Franklin is the first thing that came to my mind as I sit down to write this. It is a saying that applies to many aspects of life, including time travel. The idea of traveling through time has captivated humans for ages. From H.G. Wells' "The Time Machine" to the "Back to the Future" trilogy, the idea of traveling through time has intrigued us and made us wonder what would happen if we ever did it. The extraordinary book "The Book Of Michael - Sevenfold Doctrine" will capture your attention and make you reevaluate your views. The author has a remarkable ability to tell stories that keep readers interested and make them think.

The author, Michael Harris, discusses his intellectual exploration, which has taken him from seeing a UFO land to exploring the enigmas of telepathy and time travel. He encourages us to join him on his journey for greater knowledge by presenting difficult questions about the nature of reality and our role in the universe. People have scoured ancient books for hidden clues and mysteries throughout history. Scholars, theologians, and seekers of all stripes have long been fascinated by and inspired by the Bible because of its extensive history and everlasting wisdom. Many people's imaginations have been captured by The Bible Code; a rumored code supposedly concealed within the text of the Bible. They have considered the nature of reality and the significance of divine intervention in our lives as a result.

Michael discusses the arguments in favor of and against the existence of the Bible Code, as well as the potential implications for our understanding of the Bible. He provides a novel perspective on this contentious and complicated topic. Using a variety of sources, including biblical studies, history, and philosophy, he provides a comprehensive and meticulous explanation for this extraordinary event. Whether you are a believer, skeptic, scholar, or layperson, this book will undoubtedly challenge your preconceived notions and deepen your comprehension of the Bible and its numerous mysteries. He looks into concepts like telepathy, time travel, and resurrection.

Additionally, he uses information from numerous religious books to back up his claims. Additionally, the book delves into the idea of a moneyless system and how it might be implemented in society.

Time travel and its consequences for history are one of the book's primary subjects. Michael fights that various individuals and gatherings have used time travel to modify the direction of occasions since forever ago. He shows how time travel has changed the past by referencing events like the Flood and the resurrection of the dead. The book discusses telepathy as an important concept. He defines telepathy as the capacity to communicate without the use of words or hand gestures. He imagines that clairvoyance might be developed as a characteristic ability with training. Additionally, he argues that telepathic communication can be used to improve social cohesion. In a society where the idea of telepathy might seem like a far-fetched concept, this book forces us to reevaluate our understanding of this phenomenon and its potential effects on human contact and relationships. The author conveys his views clearly and concisely throughout the entire book. It is simple for readers to follow since he backs up his claims with examples and data. Despite the complexity of the subjects discussed in the book, Michael does a great job breaking them into manageable chunks.

One potential criticism of the book is that some readers may find Michael's theories too far-fetched. The ideas presented in the book are outside the mainstream, and some readers may find them difficult to accept. However, the author's use of evidence and reasoned justifications helps in assuaging some of these worries. The book is approachable to a broad audience due to the author's entertaining and simple-to-understand writing style. He skillfully combines a gripping tale with a thorough investigation of philosophical and theological ideas, leaving readers thinking about the book's ramifications long after reading it.

A book's defining traits are its accuracy and spontaneity, and these are what make a good book truly exceptional. Michael's book embodies these qualities, and that's why I heartily urge everyone interested in digging into the mysteries of existence to read "The Book Of Michael - Sevenfold Doctrine." This book is thought-provoking and intellectually engaging, in addition to being amusing. It is incredible how the author's different view on time travel and how it may affect people. This book is a must-read for anyone who wants to deepen their understanding of the universe and themselves. This book will give you a sense of wonder and excitement in our universe, and I guarantee you will enjoy it. So get a copy of this book and prepare to be surprised and challenged as you traverse time and space.

Elsibeth Hoyt

PREFACE

After I saw the ship, it didn't take long for me to forget, never spoke of it, as if the UFO landing didn't matter or exist. And such was my attitude at times probably not believing in God going the way of the world. But I tell you the time came when, when I did remember I was in the sorry state of Telepathy. Being so deep those on the other side knew me. I was like the walker who came to the other side they could not wake up.

A day came they told me they would send me bad dreams to scare me awake. But they said I was so deep they could not scare me awake. I walked among them; I suppose. Many time they spoke of me as if I was the intruder as if I could see them who could not be seen. So, began my turn towards UFOs. It was not long before I realized I was dealing with an intelligence on the other side more advanced than we.

Thus began my study, I first conceived the thought to find the "War in Heaven". I thought if I found the War in Heaven, I would find UFOs. I thought there was no way to fight a War in Heaven without a ship. So, I started there. But quickly realized it was not in the Bible, yet the Bible talked about something I couldn't find it? So, what turned out to be a pursuit into research in which led to the realization of telepathy, Time travel and other mysteries.

Why Telepathy Should Be Taught?

Telepathy: can best be described as a human rights issue. It's basically a fact that if two or more people think and feel the same thought at the same time.
Best shown by example:
1- If a civilian and and a police officer are involved in a dispute which leads to violence.
(A) the police thinks to strike the man, the man thinking the same exact thought at the same exact time thinks to strike the police.
Comment: both men are thinking the exact same thought at the same time. One man having more authority wrongly accuses one of a crime. The innocent man feels justified at proclaiming his innocence being attack. Thinking he is wrongly accused and attacked. While at the same time attacking. The police feel, this criminal is violent while attacking.

- Telepathy is not the fault of the receiver of that thought, the fault lies with the sender of the thought. By Gods law, as well as the false accuser's fault. Though things are based on the law which gives the police the authority, the falsely accusing makes him wrong.

Accusation is based on not knowing the truth and acting as if you know the truth when you don't. Yet, these many wrongs go uncorrected if a society is based on a presidency of falsely accusing to find the truth. But the accusations falsely is a crime against God.

"And I heard a loud voice saying in heaven, Now is come salvation, and strength, and the kingdom of our God, and the power of his Christ: for the accuser of our brethren is cast down, which accused them before our God Day and night."
Revelation 12:10 KJV

Accusation is not knowing, not knowing is based on correctly viewing what one perceives or thinks. Telepathy is the teaching of one. So, if you have one teaching and one way you.

Now, having one way, creates a single measure to measure all things by. Why do we measure? We measure to equal divide so no person feels they are less than another.

Any time you create class systems you eliminate equality and nothing you think is equal, this is the fact. Different strokes for different folks. Rich and poor all these problems which never get solved are implemented in the earth.

So, your law makers give some more and some less by design. Thereby creating inequality as a standard in this system. Which will primarily rely on brute force. Having so many problems creating new problems.

The poor needing more but given less, think of other ways of survival leading to other crime, drugs, sex, murder, riff raff of all types. So, those having more, want more giving less becomes a cycle.

Example: Let's say a woman wrongly accused a man of a thought. Oh, he offended me by thinking this thought. And the man says to those people I did not think that thought about this woman. Further I have no desire to think this thought about the woman.

Well, we say you did think this thought further we will punish you according to thinking that thought. Now this is a way, founded in psychology. So, psychology requires some bases in fact. But the basis of that fact is not founded on fact but a way.

Our way is to accuse and while accusing start punishments even though he may not be wrong. But when released and he, lost his job, his wife, his possession.

Having nothing, they turn their backs and act as if it's his fault, but having nothing to do with it, is wrongly accused and those accusing feel justified in their wrongness being wrong. Again brut force is on of governance of the people, having laws with wrongs not justified or corrected as an outcome.

Well of course all these things imply the persons have little meaning by class. Such things might not exist in one class not being equal. Yet, these deem themselves above any standard of the law, with power to change the law making more unequal laws.

If a dog or a dolphin sniff a woman's private area and the woman think it funny. The God put the exact same thought in a man. And the man acknowledged to that woman the same feeling and touching her. The woman becomes offended.

Say this man brutally groped me, and so humiliated me, by his touching of me. And I am so distraught. Telepathy is that same thought the animal thought, yet the results are different.

The man being singled out by a teaching which caused women not to treat men like animals. So, the teaching put in the woman, has caused her to turn on the men, but not those animals, the animals made her happy doing the same. And if anyone believes teachings are not responsible for this action, you are sadly mistaken. Had some of these teachings been employed against races, these same independence movements could be seen as racist. This law or teaching is

So, by looking at this we can see the natural state of a woman not taught to be against something. And the other is the effect of that teaching on a woman which causes her to single out that man, for punishment.

"For the word of God is quick, and powerful, and sharper than any two-edged sword, piercing even to the dividing asunder of soul and spirit, and of the joints and marrow, and is a discerner of the thoughts and intents of the heart."
Hebrews 4:12 KJV

in·tent
/inˈtent/
noun
intention or purpose.

Okay, let's say UFOs are monitoring Telepathy which the books say they are. So, if you see, the word of God that man's intent was not the thought the woman thought and those people against the man. But that was those people way, which is wrong.

Evidence says God can putt a man's heart in a beast and a man's heart in a beast and the beast heart into a man.
Example:

So, Gods seems to be able to join us with beast of the field and other things through some Telepathic means.
"let his heart be changed from man's, and let a beast's heart be given unto him; and let seven times pass over him."
Daniel 4:16 KJV

So, here with Balaam, we see the ass speaking like a man with a man's heart. I show you these point to say. What if God is putting the exact same thought from the dog or dolphin in a man to show and see what the effects are of a teaching which teaches woman to be against men. For their own ambition, but what if God is measuring these things for judgment day. So, let's say that woman has claimed sexual harassment or wrongly touching and accusing that man. So, if God took the same thought and put it in one or the other to measure the response or effects from a teaching on a woman.
"And the ass said unto Balaam, Am not I thine ass, upon which thou hast ridden ever since I was thine unto this day? was I ever wont to do so unto thee? And he said, Nay."
Numbers 22:30 KJV

Jubilees

And on that day on which Adam went forth from the garden, he offered as a sweet savour an offering, frankincense, galbanum, and stacte, and spices in the morning with the rising of the sun from the day when he covered his shame. 28. And on that day was closed the mouth of all beasts, and of cattle, and of birds, and of whatever walketh, and of whatever moveth, so that they could no longer for they had all spoken one with another with one lip and with one tongue.

"And I will give them one heart, and I will put a new spirit within you; and I will take the stony heart out of their flesh, and will give them an heart of flesh:"
Ezekiel 11:19 KJV

Who do you think this prophet of God speaks of.

Evidence is clear humans' animals, and all things are connected from a single spirit giving all one understanding. So, it's my belief UFO monitor this spirit, and probably can manipulate it.
So, as they can see through the eyes of animal's insects other by joining all their understanding together. Certainly, one day as my dog walked me to the back door and I went it. I saw him suddenly turn and knew he went to drink water. I turned around snuck out of the house to go outside and see him drinking. I went out he was drinking, so is thought it's all relative. We all see the same by our Telepathic transmissions.
So, it's also possible they spy on us through these other life forms on Earth monitoring all things. I think Telepathy is a side effect of this spirit which joins all things together.
This is two men having Telepathy, in Daniels book Susanna, whom I must also note both me and the prophet Daniel studied the same thing in Telepathy. But pretty sure its that spirit joined all the animals together and man with them with one tongue I saw spirit. It's confirmed!
Susanna
And the one said to the other, let us now go home: for it is dinner time.
So, when they were gone out, they parted the one from the other, and turning back again they came to the same place; and after that they had asked one another the cause, they acknowledged their lust: then appointed they a time both together, when they might find her alone.

This is a man and a woman having Telepathy. They are believed to be in a Trance up to this point tied into the spirit which joined all things together be this example given. Adam and Eve
"And they were both naked, the man and his wife, and were not ashamed."
Genesis 2:25 KJV
"And the eyes of them both were opened, and they knew that they were naked; and they sewed fig leaves together and made themselves aprons."
Genesis 3:7 KJV

So, the moral of our story is, I can create a way and teaching Telepathy which would join as one and cause all to have Telepathy. From my Archangel study it is possible. The Teaching of one way to create one understanding in all things. Yes, it's a formula to take a species such as ours. And teach them all Telepathy. Through designs and arrangements of physical things making all the relative to another to the most minute detail, in a repetitive way throughout all design.

Let's look at God.

Most don't know I considered fashion. 1977 i started going to the Presidio in San Francisco to watch the women at Letterman Army Hospital do shows and Fashion shows.
So, a little later taking models to Las Vegas when I did shows. So, I asked a girl to see her dress she was going to show everyone anyway, she walked around the job all day it was no secret. See wasn't wearing her jacket all day in the office, she took it off. I simply meant to open it up to see it. There is accusation of sexual comment as my intent.
Key word: Intent, I asked the girl to see her dress. Intent: sexual remark or style-based question. What God says about intent?
"For the word of God is quick, and powerful, and sharper than any two-edged sword, piercing even to the dividing asunder of soul and spirit, and of the joints and marrow, and is a discerner of the thoughts and intents of the heart."
Hebrews 4:12 KJV

in·tent
/inˈtent/
noun
intention or purpose.

Discerner of thoughts and intent

Twenty-five years ago, this happened, and it was a lie then and a lie now. I had zero interest in her as a female. By the same token God might have an example of her allowing someone to say something offensive and get away with it due to her belief system.
"And I will give them one heart, and I will put a new spirit within you; and I will take the stony heart out of their flesh, and will give them an heart of flesh:"
Ezekiel 11:19 KJV

Who do you think this prophet of God speaks of.
   Evidence is clear humans' animals, and all things are connected from a single spirit giving all one understanding. So it's my belief UFO monitor this spirit, and probably can manipulate it. So, as if they can see through the eyes of animal's insects other by joining all their understanding together. So, it's also possible they spy on us through these other life forms on Earth monitoring all things. I think Telepathy is a side effect of this spirit which joins all things together. I believe I saw this spirit and have positively discovered and identified it also found in the books of God.
   You can go farther and say what was the man's intent? A man puts his hand on your waist to guild you through the door first, being a gentleman. (His intent) What was the woman's intent? Oh, he touched me inappropriately! What is her intent, to hurt him, see him punished. So, who's the bad guy? Plus, she was going to walk around all day in the dress anyway, with everyone in the building seeing her in it all day long.
   So, it wasn't something that was in anyway obscene, but who would figure something which was going to happen anyway was offensive. So, this is based on Christian Law, not politics. It's Christian Law, not something politically correct. You keep your belief out of Christian Law. This isn't politics, not asking you to defend your belief by deposing mine. This isn't politics. It's based on human rights. When you make laws which give you no legal defense. It's actually a judgment before any trial. And to me unconstitutional, because the law is designed not to be defendable, but flatly makes all the accused guilty without trial. Even if they aren't! Really one of the worst of

unfair laws. And let this complaint stand because you are not perfect, you are not without fault. And I am not going up against a perfect entity. But a entity more so built up on abuse and unfairness. One way or another, turn the tide, switch the side, it all still abuse. We should always have compassioned designed into any doctrine, look at Christ saving the woman of Adultery, that's saying you all are wrong, again what is intent. Oh you think you don't have to live with others? Just teach hate, spread a hateful way saying it makes you strong. Remember Christ in his compassion.

"So when they continued asking him, he lifted up himself, and said unto them, He that is without sin among you, let him first cast a stone at her."
John 8:7 KJV

Christ had compassion on a woman, so, simply put, women's doctrine should also hold compassion against man, to not sever the bond. Such is a teaching of man, and of women. That all teachings lead you astray. They take you down, another way.
A woman may say she has a bond with the man. But I tell you truly a teaching can spellbound you and cause you to see things a certain way. Capable of blinding you from bonding or understanding the man. Teachings can blind any to the way of any other. Teachings are the blinding of one man against the other.
Woman teachings has cause them not to understand or see a way to bond. Making it hard to also understand the man. All-natural affection for the man taught out that you do not see, you have a bond. Consider that when you say you know him! Knowing him to some might be staying away, always seeing the result.
But if we look at teaching, they ultimately cause you to see things other than your natural way of seeing things. Why is one team against another? Why when they speak a foreign language you can't understand it? I tell you why because teachings blind you to the ways of others. So, just because you once had a natural affection. You have been taught not to see it, so don't go around thinking you still have a natural bond you don't. and in seeing you don't see.

DEDICATION

I would like to thank Project Prime Marketing, for developing a system to assist writers to succeed in the field of writing and entertainment.

Second this is dedicated to people who think they know your thoughts, yet you are incapable of doing what you practice. So, many are wrongly judged by all you imagine.

This is a dedication to two or three prophets, apostles and witnesses being made credible again in the teaching of the word of God.

That Christian Law is Certified as being more credible than Canon Law which I seek to overthrow by its limitations. Which are not limitations made by God or men of God, but men.

Dedicated to the teaching of Telepathy which, if we teach one teaching to all men of earth. If that teaching is good, it makes all men of earth equal as a standard of Telepathy. It's required to be equal to see Telepathy by design. And again, special thanks to project prime marketing for this opportunity to express something close to my heart.

Special thanks to Michael Diaz for his patience with me on certain matters.

INTRODUCTION

This is the actual Bible code, and it can be proven, further goes against the current order of the Church, so the variance between Christian Law and Canon Law. And we know variance is a sin, so that Canon Law does not allow two or three Prophet, Apostles or Witnesses to speak. The books speak only what they approve to speak and that's not the teaching.

"Verily I say unto you, Whatsoever ye shall bind on earth shall be bound in heaven: and whatsoever ye shall loose on earth shall be loosed in heaven. Again, I say unto you, That if two of you shall agree on earth as touching anything that they shall ask, it shall be done for them of my Father which is in heaven."
Matthew 18:18-19 KJV

"This is the third time I am coming to you. In the mouth of two or three witnesses shall every word be established."
2 Corinthians 13:1 KJV

"For where two or three are gathered together in my name, there am I in the midst of them."
Matthew 18:20 KJV

"Let the prophets speak two or three and let the other judge."
1 Corinthians 14:29 KJV

"And the things which are therein, that there should be time no longer: but in the days of the voice of the seventh angel, when he shall begin to sound, the mystery of God should be finished, as he hath declared to his servants the prophets."
Revelation 10:1-7 KJV

So, when the church took these books and removed them and said they are not inspired of God. They themselves were not inspired by God. God was not their master in these things. Anytime you witness the dead rising and angels coming and going those very acts of God are an inspiration.

These men who reject, held to their own beliefs not of God, to hold down the word of God. With teachings in fact, which have little meaning, nor do they prove anything.

But leave me to wonder and make up what they will saying things about God not written in any book. But saying things they themselves have imagined. But all things should be done two or three.

By Prophets, Apostles and Witnesses that's the teaching. Not by things not written in any book proving God. Those things are of men and Satan, they take away books then tell you what ou can or can't say. And reason are not based on the truth but a way, so its done this way, but that way has many faults,

So when Christ told you "But I tell you of a truth, there be some standing here, which shall not taste of death, "till they see the kingdom of God." he gave you evidence of the Kingdom of God and men hid it and covered it up.

PROLOGUE

I recall one night as I slept, I saw a dark shadow the with the figure of a man standing in my room. Suddenly the dark figure came upon me. I screamed loudly waking up my mom, I would say about 1973. I kicked hard at the figure as I screamed out.

My mom ran into the room alarmed and cut on the light. I recall me and my mother were the only ones living there currently. I told her about the dark figure. I had a speaker close to the bed which I kicked so hard I broke it. Knocking the three-and-a-half-foot speaker across the room.

Some years later about four or five, while loaded with friends. Now before this, I had noticed a change in my countenance but, had not discerned what it was. While tripping caused all in the car to see altogether, seeing we all thought the same thoughts at the same time.

I pointed it out and they saw. Suddenly all in the car could not breath! All four e all at the exact same time opened all four doors and defang to jump out of the car gasping for air. They continued to go to Archie's house and try and explain what happened. Of course, everyone said what y'all tripping on. I listened and said nothing, knowing it could not be explained.

A day came after that I could not eat, and this went on a while until I became dehydrated to the point I cramped so and was in great pain Four days not sleeping. I had done some permanent nerve damage I could never run again. and had not eaten right in at least sixty days. So, being safe I should say I fasted forty days. Well, I could not eat, it was as if a spell came over.

A night came when there was a powerful electrical storm. Powerful clouds moved across the horizon spaced out across the horizon looking like warships with light striking out in five or 6 places at once. I was amazed at the power of these storms. I then dosed off and fell asleep.

While sleeping, I saw this black angel dressed in a breastplate of light come to me from a bolt of lightning which struck the earth. The Angel walked towards me as if to tell me something, but when I looked at that Angel it was me? But have ascertained I was viewing something another saw, as if we were in the same place or I walked in his shoes, on the day of the resurrection.

After that I was then taunted by spirits waking me in the night foretelling to me what I would see when opening my eyes. I was heckled by one showing me I could hear people think and foretelling me what I would see. Then I saw a UFO oval shape. The UFO was amber in color, I came upon it fast and was inside.

I came upon an Angel who was pitch black in color, wearing a hood from his clothing with dark colors and the place was dark. I came upon him so quickly he seemed startled and surprised at my coming. He began to pray to me, but when he spoke his mouth did not move! This angel was a powerful Telepathic. He pointed at a machine and gave me a choice in which way to go, that symbol the Archimedes Spiral.

I left that place quickly and passed to a place where I heard a multitude of men calling me. These men were held in great darkness and a pale green light on the horizon. I walked towards the dark place where those men's voices came from. They announced themselves to me by the thousands then a few spoke.

They were former presidents and great men of the earth. These are those held by that dark Angel, which I fled from and did not pray with him when he prayed. His hand reached out to shake my hand after he prayed, and I did not shake his hand. He became angry with me and I fled to the place of those men held in darkness.

As they spoke to me, they told me they were all wrong and asked me not to shake this dark angel's hand as they all had done. And I left that place, there was one very prominent man who asked me to deliver a more private message. But because of his stature in this world, many would come out against me. So, I would not declare the things he told me.

After this I recall a gland or something popped in the back of my head and I became telepathic. Those on the other side had warned me I had gone too deep and could see even them. When I was awake all things became out of cinque as if I knew ahead of time things, names of people and such, but clarity was very bad.

I was told to me I was like Adam and from that point forward began my research of things. I found also in the books of Adam Satan was black, blacker than we of earth. Coming from Jupiter, he was Telepathic, and they are Grigori, Satan's ship is a great light. The same, its a throne which are ships are form of the stars or big lights.

Then there came a day somewhat like other days, when I rested deeply! I heard a man's voice who talked or taught. Then after hearing him in a consistent way for some weeks. I fell into a deep rest in the middle of the day.

I was in a dark place, pitch black in my mind. Suddenly I saw a door opened, it's light on the other side. This light did not come into the darkness just a doorway into the light. While clearly hearing that man teach. So, I went through the door and was walking in what was like a cloud. I followed the man's voice into the midst, and it got closer.

I came to a place where I saw four or five men who were white, sitting in a trance looking at a place the man's voice spoke. So, I turned to see what they looked at, and soon as I looked, I went into the trance. And was taught Telepathy in a fast way, given understanding.

I snapped out of the trance and looked and saw those four or five men, maybe four, still in the trance. I looked back at the light that was in the cloud and again was in the trance being taught Telepathy.

After this, I came out of the trance and saw two men standing to the right of that light in the cloud and those four men sitting still in that trance. Those two men asked me if I could see them. I told them yes; I can see you. Those two asked me to repeat some things they explained to me some problems of retention with memory.

They said things like I would not remember, but they put something in me that would come out one day people would believe what I said. They told me I did not belong in that place and must leave. I told them I did not want to leave because I liked the Telepathy they taught.

They told me to look at the cloud and pointed behind me. I turned and looked, they asked what did I see I told them, I see my friend Archie and going to the gym to play basketball. They told me I must go and remember what they taught, and told me one day they would return. Then I heard the white ones speak, as did we all speak in one voice at the same time.

They told me to wake up and remember all they had taught me. Then I awoke and it was in the fall of the year. And I heard leaves which crackled from footsteps that approached the house after a short while, while I contemplated. I heard the knock at the door. I got up and opened it, it was my friend Archie and he asked if I wanted to go to the gym to play basketball.

I responded no and did not and nor had we any immediate plans to go to that gym. I recall he had mentioned it about two weeks prior, since I had been out of state a while. I had recently returned home after a year and a half or so, so going to the gym was not a practice of mine.

EPIGRAPH

8 millennium compressed into 1000 years this is the formula to raise the dead. (or stop all time to raise the dead)

    (A) 7 millennium running concurrently
        as one millennium.
    (B) but dead might be raised, spread out over
        a thousand years rising on the 8 Day.
    (C) weather and elements will become more
        extreme, electrical clouds 7 times more
        powerful.
    (D) 7 atmospheres combine into one, causing
        conditions to become extreme to the
        point of destruction of the earth.
    (E) the sun 7 times brighter, because Time is
        Stuck Together in the most literal sense
    (F) the earth opening seemingly to its
        core, earthquakes opening deep.
        recesses of the earth.
    (G) Kingdom of Heaven is here, upon the
        earth and we are becoming as angels.

9 Or 9000 years would be equal to 1000 years, Time Stuck together.
10 Or the "Eighth Day"

And the Aeon by its description, no time, to say, I could step in and out of time, to different points in time.

EYE'S OPENED

I think the next day while I sat on the front porch. While I was sitting, I thought of two young men I did not know. These two young men, I had seen also about two weeks before. And I thought why did I think of these two young men I did not know? So, I thought, they must be coming down the street like before when I saw them last.

So, I got up to look and could not see up the street because of a hedgerow which ran out to the street from my neighbor's house. So, after standing up I went out to the sidewalk to look up the street and saw clearly those two young men I saw weeks before having thought of them as if we all have a presence which announces itself to us before your coming. thought of again walking down the street toward me.

I guess what I supposed in all this, was it possible something possessed me. Or was a part of me taken from me when that ship came, and then taught me, and put that part back in me in that storm. And caused me to see Satan, the Grigori before I learned these things in the books.

Or how did I know Adam was a Telepathic who fasted, teaching his children. Later that became the teachings of the prophets. These are the things which led me, where I went in my study.

Did I stand in a place with Gods Holy Seven angels? Or was I the seventh Angel, because when I counted those outside that light there were seven or eight. So, it was as if I stood with Michael and his Angels, even before I studied from the books and knew these things. It was as if I knew it's all ahead of my learning. Even forty years.

And remember this, I heard the man teach after that one time but seemed far away. But they all told me one day they would return. Of course, there are other things I didn't write, but for now. Study of Telepathy

Look at the definition of Telepathy, they are casting doubt it exist at the same time it's being defined. They are programming people not to believe in it even in the definition of it.

te·lep·a·thy
/təˈlepəTHē/
noun
the supposed communication of thoughts or ideas by means other than the known senses.

sup·posed
/səˈpōzd/
adjective
generally assumed or believed to be the case, but not necessarily so.

So, it's man's psychology to cast doubt so as to control by other means peoples thoughts being led by teachings. So, the very definition is tainted with a false and misleading viewpoint. It's basically a coverup where these things are being twisted to mean other things. Fact is Telepathy is naturally occurring thing in humanity and life. Something which happens naturally yet is covered up. Teachings made up mean more than something which happens in us naturally, yet its covered up and used against use to control us.

So, this warrants a coverup. To show, they are misleading people as to the true nature of what Telepathy is. It does not mean you are a mind reader. Nor does it necessarily mean you think you know what others are thinking. But, that it's the ability to show transmissions between people and other.

The origin of the teaching of Telepathy on earth and one way to achieve it as I myself have learned the hard way like Adam. Unintended lesson in my case I seemly stumbled on to it but in fact, I believe I was driven to it by outside forces such as UFO's.

1st Book of Adam and Eve 8

2 Then God the Lord said unto Adam, "When thou wast under subjection to Me, thou hadst a bright nature within thee, and for that reason couldst thou see things afar off. But after thy transgression thy bright nature was withdrawn from thee; and it was not left to thee to see things afar off, but only near at hand; after the ability of the flesh; for it is brutish."

1st Book of Adam and Eve 60

THEN on the eighty-ninth day, Satan came to the cave, clad in a garment of light, and girt about with a bright girdle.

2 In his hands was a staff of light, and he looked most awful: but his face was pleasant and his speech was sweet,

3 He thus transformed himself in order to deceive Adam and Eve, and to make them come out of the cave, ere they had fulfilled the forty days.

4 For he said within himself, "Now that when they had fulfilled the forty days' fasting and praying, God would restore them to their former estate; but if He did not do so, He would still be favorable to them; and even if He had not mercy on them, would He yet give them something from the garden to comfort them; as already twice before."

So, what you are witnessing is the teaching of Telepathy being established by Adam the First Man. He's teaching us how to contact UFO's which few men today believe exists.

1st Book of Adam and Eve 29

5 And Adam wept before the Lord God and begged and entreated Him to give him something from the garden, as a token to him, wherein to be comforted.

6 And God looked upon Adam's thought, and sent the angel Michael as far as the sea that reaches unto India, to take from thence golden rods and bring them to Adam.

Noah the Telepathic: point why would the other sons walk into the room backwards so as not to see him when they covered him? What were they afraid of? It's obvious he's a Telepathic to put fear such as this within then.

Plus, why did Noah think it was Shem, since Shem's garment was upon him?

Jubilees 7 (written 2 or 3 times)
And it was evening, and he went into his tent, and being drunken he lay down and slept, and was uncovered in his tent as he slept. And Ham saw Noah his father naked and went forth and told his two brethren without. And Shem took his garment and arose, he and Japheth, and they placed the garment on their shoulders and went backward and covered the shame of their father, and their faces were backward. And Noah awoke from his sleep and knew all that his younger son had done unto him, and he cursed his son and said: "Cursed be Canaan; an enslaved servant shall he be unto his brethren."

"And Ham, the father of Canaan, saw the nakedness of his father, and told his two brethren without. And Shem and Japheth took a garment, and laid it upon both their shoulders, and went backward, and covered the nakedness of their father; and their faces were backward, and they saw not their father's nakedness. And Noah awoke from his wine and knew what his younger son had done unto him."
Genesis 9:22-24 KJV

I am not saying Telepathy may not cause other problems, it does. Particularly if you don't know it's Telepathy and you're being told by non-Telepathic people it's something else, or by those who cover it up through deception such as the definition of it.

The Secrets of Enoch 1
5 And when I was asleep, great distress came up into my heart, and I was weeping with my eyes in sleep, and I could not understand what this distress was, or what would happen to me.
6 And there appeared to me two men, exceeding big, so that I never saw such on earth; their faces were shining like the sun, their eyes too were like a burning light, and from their lips was fire coming forth with clothing and singing of various kinds in appearance purple, their wings were brighter than gold, their hands whiter than snow.
7 They were standing at the head of my couch and began to call me by my name.

8 And I arose from my sleep and saw clearly those two men standing in front of me.

So, I myself am like those Telepath's, well as I laid sleep and my mother came into the room looked at the clock and I saw what Time it was. I woke up went to look at the clock she looked at and saw the time I dreamed of, while seeing her look at the clock when I awoke.
Are the time I was warned in a dream by those six or seven angels which I was among or one of. That my friend Archie approached. And I knew what he would say when he came. No, but I am not a mind reader, but that does not mean I am not affected by transmissions of those around me. Recall Christ with Nathanael? How he told him he saw him sitting under the fig tree? That was Telepathy and Nathanael immediately knew of his gift and what was in Christ. So, with many others like Samuel, and the profits of old.

"Philip findeth Nathanael, and saith unto him, we have found him, of whom Moses in the law, and the prophets, did write, Jesus of Nazareth, the son of Joseph. And Nathanael said unto him, Can there any good thing come out of Nazareth? Philip saith unto him, Come and see. Jesus saw Nathanael coming to him, and saith of him, behold an Israelite indeed, in whom is no guile! Nathanael saith unto him, whence knowest thou me? Jesus answered and said unto him, before that Philip called thee, when thou wast under the fig tree, I saw thee. Nathanael answered and saith unto him, Rabbi, thou art the Son of God; thou art the King of Israel. Jesus answered and said unto him, Because I said unto thee, I saw thee under the fig tree, believest thou? Thou shalt see greater things than these."
John 1:45-50 KJV

EPIGRAPH

Telepathy

So, this one is a lobby security desk with two identical phones in every way. Both had two incoming phone lines with the same extension so both phones could be accessed from a broad location in association with cameras, gate controls alarm panels for gasses and such.

2 incoming lines, corporate emergency line, ring down line for gates and dock, controls for delivery traffic from afar. spare lines.

So, the security officer next to me operated the gate. No one at the guard shack, I was on Patrol and just came in. I sat down in front of the other phone a few four feet apart from her. I was catching up on my log, writing.

So, she was corresponding with Shipping and Receiving because a truck came. Now, all she was doing was accomplished. Normally at that time they would put the phone extension on incoming calls. This was so you did not accidentally ring shipping and receiving, creating a situation of dealing both with internal and outside calls which were frequent.

Now about a few minutes had past, and normally that means you forgot to change the extension to prevent accidentally calling shipping and receiving because soon as you pick up the phone to answer it you are calling shipping. Now, you change the extension to answer the incoming call. But now shipping is calling you back forcing you to put the outside call on hold. So, to prevent we just kept it on incoming calls. Because it could get busy and overwhelm.

Telepathy - Suddenly she reached for her phone to switch the extension. But, at the same time I reached for my phone to change my extension.

But I caught myself, because my phone wasn't affected. It was on an incoming call line already.

It was not even my thought but hers. I used to call those things metamorphosis.

met·a·mor·pho·sis

/ˌmedəˈmôrfəsəs/

noun

metamorphosis

a change of the form or nature of a thing or person into a completely different one, by natural or supernatural means.

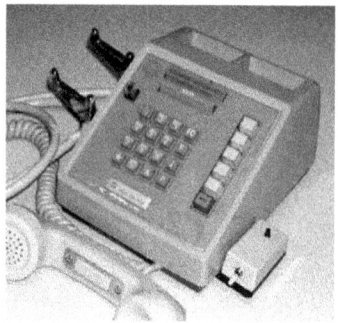 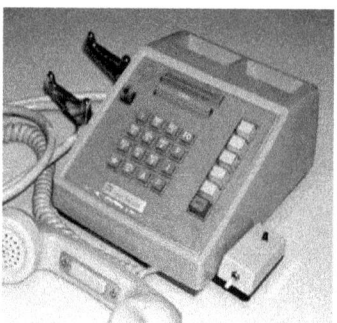

Telepathy: I noted that eating out of one plate causes people to think about grabbing the same pieces of food at the same time. Two of the exact same things can also join.

CHAPTER 01
OPENING PAGE - POSSIBLE CONTACT

Before I get into this, let me say my brother also prayed with me at the start. He also said back when in college driving from California to Oklahoma going to OSU Oklahoma State University. He was sleeping along the highway taking a break at night and sleeping. He was awakened by a light passing low over his car. He said he tried to raise up, but something seemed to hold him down. When he did raise up, he saw a light moving away low to the ground.

I suppose I should start at the beginning, when as a child, I don't know ten or so. After me and my brother and cousin had saw an article about possible UFOs in the Bible.

This had interested me more than anything else at that time about God being raised in the church. I prayed sincerely to God and his angels asking them to teach me Telepathy and show me a ship. I guess I did this for some nights.

After some years, my mother and two sisters came home from church one weekday. As we hurried towards the house to try and catch Star Trek which at the time was a series. Star Trek played until 1969, so, the UFO filmed over Winnipeg, Manitoba I am not sure of the year.

I was thinking the Winnipeg, Manitoba ship was the ship I saw landed at this time. Why the ship I saw had a signature of red white and disappearing like the Manitoba ship I think is quite unique.

Well, why is that important? It could determine the year we saw the ship landed on Joseph Weller School across from the house. Why that ship, I believe when it aired the ship changed colors from red to white and blinking out as it flew. The current film does not show color changing, because of its age.

So, my sister then spoke out and said look at the big red light on the school. We all looked for a while unsure of what it was. They all continued in the house but I continued to watch. I took a seat on the porch.

The light after a couple of minutes turns from red to white. I ran into the house and told my sisters and mom. Irene came and looked I think the others remained uninterested. Irene went back into the house. The ship then appeared to vanish, I ran into the house and announced that.

Maybe a sister came and left back into the house. I continued to sit as if I knew it was still there. It reappeared red, and white and vanished, staying in each cycle of light a couple of minutes. This went on close to half hour.

I recall after that I became very tired. So tired I went into the house and straight to bed, falling into a deep sleep. After that, I always seemed to be unsure what the thing was I never saw fly.

"While Peter thought on the vision, the Spirit said unto him, Behold, three men seek thee. Arise therefore, and get thee down, and go with them, doubting nothing: for I have sent them."
Acts 10:19-20 KJV

I will add, me and Archie would have some strange telepathic events. Things as simple as both our hands bumping trying to change the radio channel. All of us suddenly rolling down the window at the same time which was electric and stopping with the same gap in the opening of those two windows.

Then there were those five or six occurrences when without phone calls and planning, we would meet coming to one another's house in between each other's houses. Then there was the time when we changed the direction of our walking and still ran into each other halfway there.

We would play chess a lot of times. I recall a day when he was studying his move and I kind of drifted off in a day type dream. I saw something moving in the corner of my eye then looked, saw the figure of his arm moving being projected ahead of him moving. Then in about the same moment saw him move the exact move which was projected.

Funny thing is, Archie saw the 1973 UFO which passed over the neighborhood. We talked about these things quite a bit. So, I eventually pulled the news articles of his sighting, my ship was stealth like. Leaving the school, it jumped from one side of Dixon Road to the other. Dixon is a long street in which many would have been able to see it. But it jumped, moving through a row of houses on either side of the Hetch Hetchy.

I guess the first place is with me, my story and why I'm doing the sevenfold doctrine of the whole creation. What that is, is a teaching and way which is prophesied to come into existence in the latter part of the seventh millennium.

We are currently in the latter part of the seventh millennium and I'm attempting to start to teach this teaching according to this prophecy. Here, look at Daniel 12:4, it's saying we won't understand until the end.

Enoch 92
12 Afterwards, in the seventh week, a perverse generation shall arise; abundant shall be its deeds, and all its deeds perverse. During its completion, the righteous shall be selected from the everlasting plant of righteousness; and to them shall be given the **sevenfold doctrine of his whole creation.**

"But thou, O Daniel, shut up the words, and seal the book, even to the time of the end: many shall run to and fro, **and knowledge shall be increased."**
Daniel 12:4 KJV

Well, here's the thing, if we couldn't understand utill the end, how did those who removed all the books of God understand what they were doing? If they did not actually understand or know what they were doing? It does say knowledge will be increased.

The reason I say that is in many cases the things the early church removed is in fact the very things you need to understand what you would be understanding in the last day. Looking at the Book of Enoch chapter 92, we see the teaching Daniel speaks of.

Looking at the last line, we see the title of my book and what it might imply **"The Sevenfold Doctrine"** I believe a teaching of resurrection, time travel, telepathy, a moneyless system and the second coming of Christ and his angels. So, these are some of the things we will try and understand.

In this case the seventh week is the seventh millennium from the time Adam was placed in the garden and God cast him out into the earth and his wife Eve. This teaching concerns the end and where God comes from and how once in power, jumped back in time and created the heavens and the earth that we see today.

Gods coming from the future, going back before all things are created, and erased reality. Then started all over again.

Sevenfold Doctrine of The Whole Creation
Well, it's my belief after the seven millennium are stuck together there are effects in the earth which will change the physical as we know. So, they can join weather and elements together from a seven-millennium period. And moving those weathers and elements through time to other period of time to a current or past period of time to change the world as they see fit or terraform, change alter or destroy.

TIME TRAVEL
Time Being Stuck Together To Cause The Resurrection.
Is, taking at least 7 millennium of earth history and sticking it together like a single day. Opening the bottomless pit could be all life being raised for billions of years. Pretty sure that's why angels are needed to contain whatever ever is brought back. The eighth days are those of earth for seven millennium being raised best as I can determine. This opening up causes all who lived in different periods of time to be reborn or regenerated from the earth somehow.

Barnabas 13

Begin the eighth day, that is, the beginning of the other world.

10 For which cause we observe the eighth day with gladness, in which Jesus rose from the dead; and having manifested himself to his disciples, ascended into heaven.

Secret of Enoch 33

AND I appointed the eighth day also, that the eighth day should be the first-created after my work, and that the first seven revolve in the form of the seventh thousand, and that at the beginning of the eighth thousand there should be a time of not-counting, endless, with neither years nor months nor weeks nor days nor hours.

Esdras 4:37

By measure hath he measured the times; and by number hath he numbered the times; and he doth not move nor stir them, until the said measure be fulfilled.

Definition of the word Stir.

/stər/

Learn to pronounce

verb

1. move a spoon or other implement around in (a liquid or other substance) in order to mix it thoroughly.

"stir the batter until it is just combined"

Similar:

mix

blend

agitate

2. move or cause to move slightly.

Similar:

move slightly

change one's position

a slight physical movement.

3.a commotion.

move

/mo͞ov/

verb

past tense: moved; past participle: moved

1.go in a specified direction or manner; change position.

EPIGRAPH

Study of Telepathy

"While Peter thought on the vision, the Spirit said unto him, Behold, three men seek thee. Arise therefore, and get thee down, and go with them, doubting nothing: for I have sent them."
Acts 10:19-20 KJV

Unto whom it was revealed, that not unto themselves, but unto us they did minister the things, which are now reported unto you by them that have preached the gospel unto you with the Holy Ghost sent down from heaven, which things the angels desire to look into."
1 Peter 1:12 KJV

"This is he, that was in the church in the wilderness with the angel which spake to him in the mount Sina, and with our fathers: who received the lively oracles to give unto us:"
Acts 7:38 KJV

IF you notice the saying to say, the angels look into things like Telepathy and such, it's your choice to accept that.

Note: Make a mental that the angels look into (investigate); and if angel fly UFOs, UFOs will look into it. These are things which cannot be learned from the Church. When UFOs are a part of their teaching, yet they reject it.

CHAPTER 2
TIME STUCK TOGETHER

Point is not only is time effected and stuck together but all physical things will be changed as the result. And all those things of prophecy the books of God spoke of, will only then happen. All men teaching these things are happening now lead you away from the truth of what's written.

EFFECTS ON PLANTS

This is the effect of Time stuck together on plants. That plant is sprouting continuously noting motion in its rate of speed. The books are pointing out things for you particularly in the future to understand. To try and determine what is transacting. But you all chose not to believe nothing the books say thinking yourselves smart, and smarter. observe so don't believe those which say these things are in effect today.

con·tin·u·ous
/kənˈtinyəwəs/
See definitions in:
All
Mathematics
Grammar
adjective
1.forming an unbroken whole; without interruption.

EFFECTS ON PLANTS

Enoch 25
1 From thence I proceeded to the middle of the earth, and beheld a happy and fertile spot, which contained branches **continually sprouting** from the trees which were planted in it. There I saw a

holy mountain, and underneath its water on the eastern side, which flowed towards the south. I saw also on the east another mountain as high as that; and between them there were deep, but not wide valleys.

2 Water ran towards the mountain to the west of this; and underneath there was likewise another mountain.

3 There was a valley, but not a wide one, below it; and in the midst of them were other deep and dry valleys towards the extremity of the three. All these valleys, which were deep, but not wide, consisted of a strong rock, with a tree which was planted in them. And I wondered at the rock and at the valleys, being extremely surprised.

Secrets of Enoch 64

TIME STUCK TOGETHER TO CAUSE THE FLOOD

Jasher 6

11 And on that day, the Lord caused the whole earth to shake, and the sun darkened, and the foundations of the world raged, and the whole earth was moved violently, and the lightning flashed, and the thunder roared, and all the fountains in the earth were broken up, such as was not known to the inhabitants before; and God did this mighty act, in order to terrify the sons of men, that there might be no more evil upon earth.

12 And still the sons of men would not return from their evil ways, and they increased the anger of the Lord at that time and did not even direct their hearts to all this.

13 And at the end of seven days, in the six hundredth year of the life of Noah, the waters of the flood were upon the earth.

14 And all the fountains of the deep were broken up, and the windows of heaven were opened, and the rain was upon the earth forty days and forty nights.

Please note the seven cataracts, this teaching is showing us what happens when they join Time together. Taking water from those in the future to cause the flood in the past with Noah.

Enoch 88

2 Again I lifted up my eyes towards heaven and saw a lofty roof. Above it were seven cataracts, which poured forth on a certain village much water.

9 Again I looked in the vision until those cataracts from that lofty roof were removed, and the fountains of the earth became equalized, while other depths were opened.

10 Into which the water began to descend, until the dry ground appeared.

There are a series of events which of events which happen when Time is stuck together. Things like the sun going dark and then lighting up to seven time as bright. The moon would be like blood and then turn around and become bright as the sun. You see these things are the eighth day and the resurrection. What you are seeing is Time being stuck together.

TIME STUCK TOGETHER TO RAISE THE DEAD

Letters of Herod and Pilot

Now when he was crucified, there was darkness over all the world, and the sun was obscured for half a day, and the stars appeared, but no lustre was seen in them; and the moon lost its brightness, as though tinged with blood; and the world of the departed was swallowed up; so that the very sanctuary of the temple, as they call it, did not appear to the Jews themselves at their fall, but they perceived a chasm in the earth, and the rolling of successive thunders. And amid this terror the dead appeared rising again, as the Jews themselves bore witness, and said that it was Abraham, and Isaac, and Jacob, and the twelve patriarchs, and Moses, and Job, who had died before, as they say, some three thousand five hundred years. And there were very many whom I myself saw appearing in the body, and they made lamentation

Point again is when we see these people from many periods of time together at the same time we know Time has been stuck together. So since should be able to prove that Time stck together would not raise the dead. Further if Time is literally stuck together what events might or might not repeat themselves.

8 Blessed are the just who shall escape the great judgement, for they shall shine forth more than the sun sevenfold, for in this world the seventh part is taken off from all, light, darkness, food, enjoyment, sorrow, paradise, torture, fire, frost, and other things; he put all down in writing, that you might read and understand.'

Prophecy

Things which happen when oxygen is increased explained.

What many don't know when time gets stuck together all things of nature will. And that plant continually sprouting, as if in fast motion.

"I am come to send fire on the earth; and what will I, if it be already kindled?"

Luke 12:49 KJV

"And after these things I saw four angels standing on the four corners of the earth, holding the four winds of the earth, that the wind should not blow on the earth, nor on the sea, nor on any tree. And I saw another angel ascending from the east, having the seal of the living God: and he cried with a loud voice to the four angels, to whom it was given to hurt the earth and the sea,"

Revelation 7:1-2 KJV

Scientists say:

In the event of doubling the oxygen levels on Earth, the most significant changes would be the speeding up of processes like respiration and combustion. With the presence of more fuel, i.e. oxygen, forest fires would become more massive and devastating. Wet vegetation would not provide protection either.

What I'm Saying

Fact is these are the things which alter seasons, crops and all things written. Any man teaching today these things are happening now, don't listen to that person.

But oxygen and elements of the air will become seven times stronger, and fires will be unable to be stopped.

Consider the effects of all things being multiplied times themselves and that is the effect of the prophecy being taught. We as modern men simply think we are smarter and those things make little since to us. But fact of the matter is, we look at all these things wrong.

Enoch 89

34 At that time likewise I perceived that one abyss was thus opened in the midst of the earth, which was full of fire.

"For a fire is kindled in mine anger, And shall burn unto the lowest hell, And shall consume the earth with her increase, And set on fire the foundations of the mountains."
Deuteronomy 32:22 KJV

in·crease
verb
/inˈkrēs/
become or make greater in size, amount, intensity, or degree.
/ˈinˌkrēs,inˈkrēs/
an instance of growing or making greater.

What they are speaking about is breaking the earth open. Opening the earth during the resurrection. They are talking about sticking seven millennium together as one period of time and all things will increase. It will open the earth and deep valleys even to the core it can break open, with more power, more everything. (Deuteronomy 32:22)

Esdras 16
14 Behold, the plagues are sent, and shall not return again, until they come upon the earth.
15 The fire is kindled, and shall not be put out, till it consume the foundation of the earth.

"Therefore, hath the curse devoured the earth, and they that dwell therein are desolate: therefore, the inhabitants of the earth are burned, and few men left."
Isaiah 24:6 KJV

"But when ye shall see the abomination of desolation, spoken of by Daniel the prophet, standing where it ought not, (let him that readeth understand,) then let them that be in Judæa flee to the mountains:"

Mark 13:14 KJV

A special note is added to someone like me who reads and would understand what is written. For the time is at hand. That person would be a prophet most likely. But Christ also would open the books. As well as Blessed is he that readeth Revelation 1:3 as well as Well as the Secrets of Enoch 34 and 48 below.

BELIEVED TO BE CHRIST

Enoch 34
2 He who raises that generation, shall reveal to them the books of thy handwriting, of thy fathers, to them to whom he must point out the guardianship of the world, to the faithful men and workers of my pleasure, who do not acknowledge my name in vain.

Secrets of Enoch 35
2 He who raises that generation, shall reveal to them the books of thy handwriting, of thy fathers, to them to whom he must point out the guardianship of the world, to the faithful men and workers of my pleasure, who do not acknowledge my name in vain.
6 Thus I make known to you, my children, and distribute the books to your children, into all your generations, and amongst the nations who shall have the sense to fear God, let them receive them, and may they come to love them more than any food or earthly sweets, and read them and apply themselves to them.

Chapter 48
7 And those who understand not the Lord, who fear not God, who accept not, but reject, who do not receive them (sc. the books), a terrible judgement awaits these.
8 Blessed is the man who shall bear their yoke and shall drag them along, for he shall be released on the day of the great judgement.

POSSIBLE PROPHET MICHAEL OR CHRIST HE READS QUESTION?

Secrets of Enoch 48

6 Thus I make known to you, my children, and distribute the books to your children, into all your generations, and amongst the nations who shall have the sense to fear God, let them receive them, and may they come to love them more than any food or earthly sweets, and read them and apply themselves to them.

7 And those who understand not the Lord, who fear not God, who accept not, but reject, who do not receive them (sc. the books), a terrible judgement awaits these.

8 Blessed is the man who shall bear their yoke and shall drag them along, for he shall be released on the day of the great judgement.

This man in Secrets of Enoch 48:7, I considered this might be another who reads, though Christ reads. I considered this person to becomes one who understands. One who is given command of the nations by his understanding of the teaching. I have considered Michael here, I can't say, just seems a possibility.

AEON

Secrets of Enoch 65

5 When all creation visible and invisible, as the Lord created it, shall end, then every man goes to the great judgement, and then all-time shall perish, and the years, and thenceforward there will be neither months nor days nor hours, they will be stuck together and will not be counted.

TIME TRAVEL

So, what all the books are describing is the manipulation of time, somehow, to the point there is no time. Revelation 10:6 no time!

"And sware by him that liveth for ever and ever, who created heaven, and the things that therein are, and the earth, and the things that therein are, and the sea, and the things which are therein, that there should be time no longer:"

Revelation 10:6 KJV

The Aeon is doing this to all things. It kind of sound like those who remained in the universe. Are put in one big ship in spirit form and they jump back to make all things vanish. What I'm saying is when they disappear, because when you go back before all things are created, they should fail to exist in reality

So going back to the eighth day you will understand the effects of what they're doing in the next verses. So, for God to make all things new perhaps we'll exist in the spirit, when all things vanish from existence.

Evidence to support no Time.
So, we see the Angel saying there would be "No Time". This happens in earths future, at which time won't matter. Because all time which ever existed in the effected time will be affected to the point of reanimation. Because endless time fails both forward in time and backward in time. Appears to be an endless time failure of years of Time, Endless Time Failure probably anything in this period is Godlike meaning thinking might be the primary mode of travel with devices.

"And sware by him that liveth for ever and ever, who created heaven, and the things that therein are, and the earth, and the things that therein are, and the sea, and the things which are therein, that there should be time no longer:"

Revelation 10:6 KJV

Point is all things in existence are affected, even the air we breathe. The water, the heavens meteorites might come out of no place suddenly because we are reliving Time which passed again now. So, if time gets stuck together, things, events of the past chould happen again as they did in those times. That is of course if Time is really being stuck together.

And my belief, this is the warning being given in these books which are in most part removed by those who did not understand what they read. Yet having the power to corrupt by their own agendas and motives not related to God in the least bit.

"And the sun was darkened, and the veil of the temple was rent in the midst."
Luke 23:45 KJV

"But in those days, after that tribulation, the sun shall be darkened, and the moon shall not give her light,"
Mark 13:24 KJV

"The earth shall quake before them; the heavens shall tremble: the sun and the moon shall be dark, and the stars shall withdraw their shining:"
Joel 2:10 KJV

"And the fourth angel sounded, and the third part of the sun was smitten, and the third part of the moon, and the third part of the stars; so as the third part of them was darkened, and the day shone not for a third part of it, and the night likewise."
Revelation 8:12 KJV

Point 2: after this, the Sun will become seven times brighter.

"Moreover, the light of the moon shall be as the light of the sun, and the light of the sun shall be sevenfold, as the light of seven days, in the day that the LORD bindeth up the breach of his people, and healeth the stroke of their wound."
Isaiah 30:26 KJV

"Thus, saith the LORD of hosts, Behold, evil shall go forth from nation to nation, and a great whirlwind shall be raised up from the coasts of the earth. And the slain of the LORD shall be at that day from one end of the earth even unto the other end of the earth: they shall not be lamented, neither gathered, nor buried; they shall be dung upon the ground."

Jeremiah 25:32-33 KJV

So, the sun is seven times brighter because seven millennium of suns are stuck together as one sun! Isaiah 30:26 again when we look at Jeremiah 25:32-33, we see the weather patterns are combining to become more extreme. That's also because of seven millennium of effects which generate weather conditions on earth, is being multiplied by seven while seven millennium are being stuck together.

I now consider that weather events which happened in the past might also happen again. Things such as meteorites, which struck, could strike again? These natural disasters could happen all at the same time. Or, because there is no time or time stuck together. Jeremiah teaches you that whirlwinds are going to be seven times worse.

There is again the possibility that we will hit with the by the same meteorite that hit the earth 6000 years ago at the time of Noah, more or less. Revelation 8:8 speaks of.

"And the second angel sounded, and as it were a great mountain burning with fire was cast into the sea: and the third part of the sea became blood;"
Revelation 8:8 KJV

"And the third angel sounded, and there fell a great star from heaven, burning as it were a lamp, and it fell upon the third part of the rivers, and upon the fountains of waters;"
Revelation 8:10 KJV

The flood will not happen again as before due to the fact the earth itself may be changed. The earth might expand due to all of the fault lines being opened. I believe its a sign the earth has been opened before. The very fact the earth is broken is evidence of the earth expansion.

So, this is the effect of the earth expanding because of extreme pressure on the earth being seven times its current pressure adding the possibility all things will become more extreme due to time being stuck together. Seven millennium of time compressed into a single moment to raise the dead.

"But when ye shall see the abomination of desolation, spoken of by Daniel the prophet, standing where it ought not, (let him that readeth understand,) then let them that be in Judea flee to the mountains:"

Mark 13:14 KJV

The point is everything the elements will grow to seven times what we see today as the result of time being stuck together. So, these books have been misinterpreted generation to generation, some books removed based on all the misinterpretations.

Esdras 15

39 And strong winds shall arise from the east and shall open it; and the cloud which he raised up in wrath, and the star stirred to cause fear toward the east and west wind, shall be destroyed.

40 The great and mighty clouds shall be puffed up full of wrath, and the star, that they may make all the earth afraid, and them that dwell therein; and they shall pour out over every high and eminent place an horrible star,

41 Fire, and hail, and flying swords, and many waters, that all fields may be full, and all rivers, with the abundance of great waters.

42 And they shall break down the cities and walls, mountains and hills, trees of the wood, and grass of the meadows, and their corn.

So, due to time being stuck together not only are the dead raised, natural disasters of the past may occur as they had during those times. And notice Christ speaks to a man throughout his lifetime this man who is recorded at the time of Enoch. If you notice Christ speaks to a man, a man who may be the son coming from the resurrection or here before the events start. Seeing there are at least two generations spoken of at the end which understand?

So, because Time is stuck together and the dead are being raised. Men who seek death won't be able to die. This is the effect of Time Stuck Together.

"And in those days shall men seek death and shall not find it; and shall desire to die, and death shall flee from them."
Revelation 9:6 KJV

Esdras 6
20 And when the world, that shall begin to vanish away, shall be finished, then will I shew these tokens: the books shall be opened before the firmament, and they shall see all together:
21 And the children of a year old shall speak with their voices, the women with child shall bring forth untimely children of three or four months old, and they shall live, and be raised up.
22 And suddenly shall the sown places appear unsown, the full storehouses shall suddenly be found empty:
23 And that trumpet shall give a sound, which when every man heareth, they shall be suddenly afraid.
24 At that time shall friends fight one against another like enemies, and the earth shall stand in fear with those that dwell therein, the springs of the fountains shall stand still, and in three hours they shall not run.

Esdras 15
49 I will send plagues upon thee; widowhood, poverty, famine, sword, and pestilence, to waste thy houses with destruction and death.
50 And the glory of thy Power shall be dried up as a flower, the heat shall arise that is sent over thee.

Point: Many today are jumping to conclusions which say, all these things are happening now. What the books are speaking of is not happening now. These are the things which happen sevenfold times themselves with the possibility, some events repeat themselves when time is stuck together.

All these things in all the books of the prophets and teaching of apostles are those things which happen seven time themselves.

But also, when they say books are opened, they speak also of Christ. But again, it's always written as if it speaks of another who reads the books.

So, it appears Christ achieved life in the Aeon, which is a state of Zero Time, maybe consisting of thought being made manifest by thought things are achieved. The steps leading to manifestation of the physical figuring how to bring things from the mind to matter or mass in a systemic way. Every step must be duplicated and proven and made fact, and provable to how all things are made. We the recipients of this existence, seems it's required to understand these things and learn all there is in these things proving things true to its degrees or perfecting truth.

The Gospel According to Mary Magdalene
AEON: Words of Christ after the resurrection.
21 The soul answered and said, what binds me has been slain, and what turns me about has been overcome,
22 and my desire has been ended, and ignorance has died.
23 In a Aeon I was released from a world, and in a Type from a type, and from the fetter of oblivion which is transient.
24 From this time on will I attain to the rest of the time, of the season, of the Aeon, in silence

EPIGRAPH

Telepathy
Time Travel solution to the problem.

The problem (beat) is evil (Or how a place prepared meaning endless period into the future) I can't say Time because time is gone. So, a place they went into the future to make not requiring time to make it.

So, to the problem Christ must jump from the furthest point in heaven from the last thing he created to create all things new, a mystery of the seven stars.

How vast is the area prepared? So that if all the universe holds has to perhaps catch this last bus? How many worlds are justified or its just one world? How many worlds would believe it will all end and if you don't come? What then Universe?

CHAPTER 3
THE KINGDOM OF GOD CAME, BUT BOOKS REMOVED

Now here's the thing, because time was stuck together Pilot saw the future. In fact, all at the time of Christ are looking at something which has not yet happened yet did. This was taking something which happens at the end and causing it to happen at the time of Christ.

And this was what Christ spoke when he said, in Luke 19:27 they at that time are shown the future. As well as the resurrection, time also was stuck together, all else are the effects of that. They are looking at time being stuck together.

Why would I say this?

EVIDENCE OF TIME STUCK TOGETHER

"But I tell you of a truth, there be some standing here, which shall not taste of death, till they see the kingdom of God."
Luke 9:27 KJV

Letters of Herod and Pilot
And the terror of the earthquake continued from the sixth hour of the preparation until the ninth hour; and when it was evening on the first day of the week, there came a sound from heaven, and the heaven became seven times more luminous than on all other days. And at the third hour of the night the sun appeared more luminous than it had ever shone, lighting up the whole hemisphere. And as lightning-flashes suddenly come forth in a storm, so there were seen men, lofty in stature, and surpassing in glory, a countless host, crying out, and their voice was heard as that of exceedingly loud thunder, Jesus that was crucified is risen again:

Evidence of time stuck together is easy to see people being raised from the dead from different periods of time. People from before the flood and after the flood.

Others like Michael and Christ are most all raised in our future. Yet because of time stuck together, they see the future in the past.

Letter of Pilot and Herod
And He that raised up all the dead and bound Hades said, say to my disciples He goeth before you into Galilee, there shall ye see Him.

And all that night the light ceased not shining. And many of the Jews died in the chasm of the earth, being swallowed up, so that on the morrow most of those who had been against Jesus were not to be found.

And amid the terror dead men were seen rising again, so that the Jews who saw it said, we beheld Abraham and Isaac, and Jacob, and the twelve patriarchs, who died some two thousand five hundred years before, and we beheld Noah clearly in the body.

Nicodemus 20
THEN the Lord holding Adam by the hand, delivered him to Michael the archangel; and he led them into Paradise, filled with mercy and glory.

"The mystery of the seven stars which thou sawest in my right hand, and the seven golden candlesticks. The seven stars are the angels of the seven churches: and the seven candlesticks which thou sawest are the seven churches."
Revelation 1:20 KJV

"And he opened the bottomless pit; and there arose a smoke out of the pit, as the smoke of a great furnace; and the sun and the air were darkened by reason of the smoke of the pit. And in those days shall men seek death and shall not find it; and shall desire to die, and death shall flee from them."

Revelation 9:2, 6 KJV

"And I saw another mighty angel come down from heaven, clothed with a cloud: and a rainbow was upon his head, and his face was as it were the sun, and his feet as pillars of fire: and cried with a loud voice, as when a lion roareth: and when he had cried, seven thunders uttered their voices.

And when the seven thunders had uttered their voices, I was about to write: and I heard a voice from heaven saying unto me, seal up those things which the seven thunders uttered, and write them not.

Now here we have the angel telling us there is no more time. This is the mystery of God. How could a man become God? You see at some point in the Future we broke the time barrier and Godship is the result. So, things men are saying we can't do today are done by us in the future.

So, we are seeing men who lived in the past being seen in the future, even Moses and Elias or Elijah the same. Even Christ tells them not to mention until after the resurrection. This is evidence of time travel from the future. At a time after men have been raised from the dead. Yet before they are raised from the dead?

"And was transfigured before them: and his face did shine as the sun, and his raiment was white as the light. And behold, there appeared unto them Moses and Elias talking with him. Then answered Peter, and said unto Jesus, Lord, it is good for us to be here: if thou wilt, let us make here three tabernacles; one for thee, and one for Moses, and one for Elias. While he yet spake, behold, a bright cloud overshadowed them: and behold a voice out of the cloud, which said, This is my beloved Son, in whom I am well pleased; hear ye him. And when the disciples heard it, they fell on their face, and were sore afraid. And when they had lifted up their eyes, they saw no man, save Jesus only. And as they came down from the mountain, Jesus charged them, saying, Tell the vision to no man, until the Son of man be risen again from the dead."
Matthew 17:2-6, 8-9 KJV

So, at that time it was no secret they were somehow involved in such activity on earth. And the people at the time widely saw this as UFO activity. But named it other than we have. Even the UFO people of the day and organizations of the day currently disseminate misinformation.

They are not going to say it's one God under any circumstance. Oh, they might say Gods, because that's misleading. They might say, where are they from? Who are they? What do they want? They will say anything but one God. Revelation 10:6 is saying they broke the time barrier which of course on the level of no time at all would raise the dead.

And the angel which I saw stand upon the sea and upon the earth lifted his hand to heaven, and swore by him that liveth for ever and ever, who created heaven, and the things that therein are, and the earth, and the things that therein are, and the sea, and the things which are therein, **that there should be time no longer:"**

Revelation 10:1, 3-6 KJV

EFFECTS OF TIME STUCK TOGETHER

"And when the seven thunders had uttered their voices, I was about to write: and I heard a voice from heaven saying unto me, seal up those things which the seven thunders uttered, and write them not."

Revelation 10:4 KJV

And again, the electrical storms and lighting will become seven time more powerful as with the winds, all things increase. In the event of doubling the oxygen levels on Earth, the most significant changes would be the speeding up of processes like respiration and combustion. With the presence of more fuel, i.e., oxygen, forest fires would become more massive and devastating. Wet vegetation would not provide protection either.

Esdras 15

61 And thou shalt be cast down by them as stubble, and they shall be unto thee as fire.

62 And shall consume thee, and thy cities, thy land, and thy mountains; all thy woods and thy fruitful trees shall they burn up with fire.

Esdras 16

4 A fire is sent among you, and who may quench it?

5 Plagues are sent unto you, and what is he that may drive them away?

6 May any man drive away an hungry lion in the wood? or may any one quench the fire in stubble, when it hath begun to burn?

15 The fire is kindled, and shall not be put out, till it consumes the foundation of the earth.

This is what science is saying would happen if oxygen doubled but what would happen if it increased seven time its normal? So those today who teach such things are happening today, mislead. None of these things will happen until Time is stuck together, and all things become seven times, more strong powerful and the dead are raised.

Esdras 15

49 I will send plagues upon thee; widowhood, poverty, famine, sword, and pestilence, to waste thy houses with destruction and death.

50 And the glory of thy Power shall be dried up as a flower, the heat shall arise that is sent over thee.

"And there shall be no night there; and they need no candle, neither light of the sun; for the Lord God giveth them light: and they shall reign for ever and ever."
Revelation 22:5 KJV

EPIGRAPH

Rendition of the facts or Time Travel, but clearly, I'm just trying to illustrate how a Time Travel System works interpreting correctly what they are saying.

Formula Zero Time to Resurrection
Probably requires 0 time for time to get stuck together with no time.
1000 years must be maintained at all the time when joining 8000 years into 1000 years. Amount of time added at an equal rate of years stuck together up to 1000 years.

Formula Time Travel, Terraforming
Resurrection
A 1000 years, and God terraforming the earth.
- divided by 7 to thin out the atmosphere
- 7 thinned out atmospheres 142.8571428571429 years, multiply 142.8571428571429 years multiplied times 7 x 7 = 7000 years of thinned out atmospheres each atmosphere 1000 years measure in Time.
This many years 142.8571428571429 times 7 = 1000 years being flowed back into reality from 7 millennium at this rate of years for a thousand years at the end equals 8000 years (or 8th Day)
8000 years Divided by 8001 years = 0.999875015623047 Time Barrier was broken. I am now outside time. (no time, I arrived before I left)
- Time Barrier Broken zero Time
1000 years divided by 1000.25 = 0.999750062484379 Time Barrier Broken
8000 divided by 8 = 1000 divided 1000.1 = 0.999900009999 Time Barrier Broken

Zero Time as a field in time, probably thought controlled place or environment. You wouldn't walk to your destinations but probably have to think your way from place to place which requires coordinates. Also it appears those I study can use the zero-time field, while in time, thinking their way place to place however they imagine.

CHAPTER 4
TIME TRAVEL & ANGELS

The Eighth Day
"And I beheld when he had opened the sixth seal, and, lo, there was a great earthquake; and the sun became black as sackcloth of hair, and the moon became as blood;"
Revelation 6:12 KJV

"And it shall come to pass in that day, saith the Lord GOD, that I will cause the sun to go down at noon, and I will darken the earth in the clear day:"
Amos 8:9 KJV

"And when I shall put thee out, I will cover the heaven, and make the stars thereof dark; I will cover the sun with a cloud, and the moon shall not give her light."
Ezekiel 32:7 KJV

"For the stars of heaven and the constellations thereof shall not give their light: the sun shall be darkened in his going forth, and the moon shall not cause her light to shine."
Isaiah 13:10 KJV

Remember Those at the Time of Christ Saw the future, when Time was stuck together
"And it was about the sixth hour, and there was a darkness over all the earth until the ninth hour."
Luke 23:44 KJV

TIME TRAVEL
The study looks at things which when you go back before things are created, they perhaps reverse engineer as you go back in time. Then cease to exist, and perhaps only in spirit. But in that form are contained, with a possibility even the invisible body of the physical is also made.

But the Book of the Revelation tells you there is no longer Time. Why, because it has been stuck together to raise the dead, and to create all things. It opened the door for a man to be God. That without time all things are possible. From the invisible things to the visible things. That The Book of Revelation is written during this time when tie is stuck together on the eighth day.

"And I saw another mighty angel come down from heaven, clothed with a cloud: and a rainbow was upon his head, and his face was as it were the sun, and his feet as pillars of fire: and he had in his hand a little book open: and he set his right foot upon the sea, and his left foot on the earth, and cried with a loud voice, as when a lion roareth: and when he had cried, seven thunders uttered their voices. And when the seven thunders had uttered their voices, I was about to write: and I heard a voice from heaven saying unto me, Seal up those things which the seven thunders uttered, and write them not. And the angel which I saw stand upon the sea and upon the earth lifted up his hand to heaven, and sware by him that liveth for ever and ever, who created heaven, and the things that therein are, and the earth, and the things that therein are, and the sea.

THOSE SENT TO TEACH IN THE 1000 YEAR PERIOD

"Blessed and holy is he that hath part in the first resurrection: on such the second death hath no power, but they shall be priests of God and of Christ and shall reign with him a thousand years."
Revelation 20:6 KJV

Undoubtedly the place Enoch is taken is some point in the future or after those of the future came back in time.
1 They raised me up into a certain place, where there was the appearance of a burning fire; and when they pleased they assumed the likeness of men.

Enoch 17
"And of the angels he saith, Who maketh his angels spirits, And his ministers a flame of fire."
Hebrews 1:7 KJV

"And the angel of the LORD appeared unto him in a flame of fire out of the midst of a bush: and he looked, and, behold, the bush burned with fire, and the bush was not consumed."

Exodus 3:2 KJV

"And when forty years were expired, there appeared to him in the wilderness of mount Sina an angel of the Lord in a flame of fire in a bush."

Acts 7:30 KJV

"For it came to pass, when the flame went up toward heaven from off the altar, that the angel of the LORD ascended in the flame of the altar. And Manoah and his wife looked on it, and fell on their faces to the ground. But the angel of the LORD did no more appear to Manoah and to his wife. Then Manoah knew that he was an angel of the LORD."

Judges 13:20-21 KJV

Now notice, the Angel that appears to Manoah and his wife says his name is a secret in part, these Angels in most cases are from the resurrection at the end. Further there may be some angels who have not yet been born, much less resurrected. But because to time travel we are seeing them giving us evidence this teaching is true.

"And the angel of the LORD said unto him, why askest thou thus after my name, seeing it is secret?"

Judges 13:18 KJV

Yet when Christ talking about a thing which hasn't yet happened tells them it happened. Why, because they are all come from the resurrection and have broken the Time Barrier.

"And Jesus answered and said unto them, Elias truly shall first come, and restore all things. But I say unto you, That Elias is come already, and they knew him not, but have done unto him whatsoever they listed. Likewise, shall also the Son of man suffer of them."

Tobit 12

14 And now God hath sent me to heal thee and Sara thy daughter in law.

15 I am Raphael, one of the seven holy angels, which present the prayers of the saints, and which go in and out before the glory of the Holy One.

But yet, much like Manoah and his wife Time Travel is being kept a secret. All these are those of the first resurrection being made ministers and flames of fire. Those sent out from the end to teach us before the end.

"And as they came down from the mountain, he charged them that they should tell no man what things they had seen, till the Son of man were risen from the dead."
Mark 9:9 KJV

Enoch 24
Lord, and the Lord spoke to me: Enoch, beloved, all thou seest, all things that are standing finished I tell thee even before the very beginning, all that I created from non-being, and visible things from invisible.
3 Hear, Enoch, and take in these my words, for not to My angels have I told my secret, and I have not told them their rise, nor my endless realm, nor have they understood my creating, which I tell thee to-day.
4 For before all things were visible, I alone used to go about in the invisible things, like the sun from east to west, and from west to east.

thing
/THiNG/
 Learn to pronounce
noun
plural noun: things
1. an object that one need not, cannot, or does not wish to give a specific name to.
2. an inanimate material object as distinct from a living sentient being.

"For by him were all things created, that are in heaven, and that are in earth, visible and invisible, whether they be thrones, or dominions, or principalities, or powers: all things were created by him, and for him:"
Colossians 1:16 KJV

So, nothing existed in spirit or invisible form after Christ jumped back in time to create all things. If you jump back before all things are created, they will vanish from existence. So, going back to the beginning when Christ becomes God.

"Who is the image of the invisible God, the firstborn of every creature for by him were all things created, that are in heaven, and that are in earth, visible and invisible, whether they be thrones, or dominions, or principalities, or powers: all things were created by him, and for him:"
Colossians 1:15-16: KJV

"And to make all men see what is the fellowship of the mystery, which from the beginning of the world hath been hid in God, who created all things by Jesus Christ:"
Ephesians 3:9 KJV

The first born is the first resurrected. What books are saying Christ is the first resurrected among men. When he comes to power he also goes back in time and creates all things. Also, my belief Christ was raised as someone else in the "Eighth Day.

The "Eighth Day" is a period when time when is stuck together. During which time there is time travel back or forward in time. So, those coming may be quite advanced in technology capable of traveling to distant futures where all things have been learned or accomplished.

Time Stuck together is what will raise the dead that's if you take the seven millennium in which man has been on earth. Stick all seven millennium together, all the dead in all seven millennium would be raised from the dead.

This person below in Levi 5 is possibly Christ, or a man raised who goes whom we don't know. Perhaps, a man we don't know who is sent back to be Christ. Why would I say that? Remember when Christ gets raised and the Apostles can't recognize him? The belief Christ is a different person than the person they all knew.

If Christ isn't raised until this time? No one else is raised until this time. Daniel describes Michael being raised with many others at the end of the eighth day. Now Christ was taken in the fifth millennium before all others! The books may be describing Michael the archangel being raised in the eighth day as well. These books also document Michael which can show time travel.

Levi 5

11 And in the seventh week shall become priests, who are idolaters, adulterers, lovers of money, proud, lawless, lascivious, abusers of children and beasts.

12 And after their punishment shall have come from the Lord, the priesthood shall fail.

13 Then shall the Lord raise up a new priest.

14 And to him all the words of the Lord shall be revealed; and he shall execute a righteous judgement upon the earth for a multitude of days.

15 And his star shall arise in heaven as of a king.

Here this is the person the many appear not to know yet is written about from the beginning. Or perhaps a man who gets resurrected in the eighth day and sent back to be Christ who Enoch described. But it appears this is not Christ true appearance changed after being resurrected perhaps is a sign the body, Christ appeared in was not the body Christ originally came in.

SUPPOSITION OF MICHAEL

I can't rightly say because if Christ is the ancient of days and the son of David, who is the other man? I do know Michael is written of; he will command the Nations? This is the resurrection of Michael, at some point after God has taken out the evil ones.

"And at that time shall Michael stand up, the great prince which standeth for the children of thy people: and there shall be a time of trouble, such as never was since there was a nation even to that same time: and at that time thy people shall be delivered, every one that shall be found written in the book.

And many of them that sleep in the dust of the earth shall awake, some to everlasting life, and some to shame and everlasting contempt. And they that be wise shall shine as the brightness of the firmament; and they that turn many to righteousness as the stars for ever and ever."
Daniel 12:1-3 KJV

Now this could be Michael or Christ, well, all seven angels are men. These seven men live, die, and are resurrected.

Esdras 1
39 Unto whom I will give for leaders, Abraham, Isaac, and Jacob, Oseas, Amos, and Micheas, Joel, Abdias, and Jonas,
49 Nahum, and Abacuc, Sophonias, Aggeus, Zachary, and Malachy, which is called also an angel of the Lord.

"And the sons of Uzzi; Izrahiah: and the sons of Izrahiah; Michael, and Obadiah, and Joel, Ishiah, five: all of them chief men."
1 Chronicles 7:3 KJV

"Thou whom I have taken from the ends of the earth, and called thee from the chief men thereof, and said unto thee, thou art my servant; I have chosen thee, and not cast thee away."
Isaiah 41:9 KJV

Pretty sure Michael and his angels are those talked about by Hermes and Enoch which in one Michael tell Enoch, Adam is his ancestor. Describes the period of 1000 years peace with Christ after the second coming. Showing us time travel, which requires deductive reasoning to see. So, the Lord speaks about those he took from the ends of the earth, at the resurrection and made them his angels calling them by name.

A MAN CLAIMED TO BE AN ANGEL

"And the LORD went before them by day in a pillar of a cloud, to lead them the way; and by night in a pillar of fire, to give them light; to go by day and night:"
Exodus 13:21 KJV

Jubilees
29. And the angel of the presence who went before the camp of Israel took the tables of the divisions of the years from the time of the creation of the law and of the testimony of the weeks, of the jubilees, according to the individual years, according to all the number of the jubilees from the day of the [new] creation when the heavens and the earth shall be renewed and all their creation according to the powers of the heaven,

Let's look at Judah's claim to be the angel of the presence, what if he was? You have a teaching saying we came from the future to save ourselves that who Christ and his angels are. These books tell some angels life stories as also came Christ. But all their story begin after the resurrection as angels who come back in time to teach and help.

Judah 4
27 And after these things shall Abraham and Isaac and Jacob arise unto life; and I and my brethren shall be chiefs of the tribes of Israel:
28 Levi first, I the second, Joseph third, Benjamin fourth, Simeon fifth, Issachar sixth, and so all in order.
29 And the Lord blessed Levi, and the Angel of the Presence, me; the powers of glory, Simeon; the heaven, Reuben; the earth, Issachar; the sea, Zebulun; the mountains, Joseph; the tabernacle, Benjamin; the luminaries, Dan; Eden, Naphtali; the sun, Gad; the moon, Asher.

The Six Men (Archangels)
Hermes Similitude 9
117 With those is the Lord encompassed as with a wall: but the gate is the Son of God, who is the only way of coming unto God. For no man shall go to God, but by his Son.

118 Thou sawest also, said he, the six men, and in the middle of them that venerable great man, who walked about the tower, and rejected the stones out of the tower?

119 Sir, said I, I saw them. He answered that tall man was the Son of God: and those six were his angels of most eminent dignity, which stand about him on the right hand and on the left.

120 Of these excellent angels none comes in unto God without him. He added, Whosoever therefore shall not take upon him his name, he shall not enter into the kingdom of God.

THE SIX MEN ARE ARCHANGELS WHEN RAISED FROM THE DEAD

Enoch 20

1 These are the names of the angels who watch.

2 Uriel, one of the holy angels, who presides over clamor and terror.

3 Raphael, one of the holy angels, who presides over the spirits of men.

4 Raguel, one of the holy angels, who inflicts punishment on the world and the luminaries.

5 Michael, one of the holy angels, who, presiding over human virtue, commands the nations.

6 Sarakiel, one of the holy angels, who presides over the spirits of the children of men that transgress.

7 Gabriel, one of the holy angels, who presides over Ikisat, over paradise, and over the cherubim. These six angels go back in Time and Raise up Enoch who is the first or seventh Angel. But Enoch is raised up after Christ come to power after the resurrection over seven millennium away.

So, during the War in Heaven Enoch is added, and before the flood, the resurrected angels are here with Christ even at the creation. Remember, time has failed and has no meaning. Enoch 89 speaks of events which take place after the resurrection and the time ship is that throne you see being built.

Enoch 89

29 And I saw a throne erected in a delectable land.

30 Upon this sat the Lord of the sheep, who received all the sealed books.

31 Which were open before him.

32 Then the Lord called the first seven white ones and commanded them to bring before him the first of the first stars, which preceded the stars whose form partly resembled that of horses; the first star, which fell down first; and they brought them all before him.
33 And he spoke to the man who wrote in his presence, (Enoch)

Who is this man? I consider Michael a possibility because he also would rule the nations.

Secrets of Enoch 48
6 Thus I make known to you, my children, and distribute the books to your children, into all your generations, and amongst the nations who shall have the sense to fear God, let them receive them, and may they come to love them more than any food or earthly sweets, and read them and apply themselves to them.
7 And those who understand not the Lord, who fear not God, who accept not, but reject, who do not receive them (sc. the books), a terrible judgement awaits these.
8 Blessed is the man who shall bear their yoke and shall drag them along, for he shall be released on the day of the great judgement.

Perhaps he's specifically a man who is one of the seven angels who would be one of the seven lamps. And once again Christ speaks to Michael and his angels.

"He that overcometh shall inherit all things; and I will be his God, and he shall be my son."
Revelation 21:7 KJV

This is Christ talking to Michael, Enoch tells you Michael would command the nations. Well, we know the seven angels are given power and thrones by what's written, but that's another story I may not get to.

"And he that overcometh, and keepeth my works unto the end, to him will **I give power over the nations:**"
Revelation 2:26 KJV

Enoch 20

5 Michael, one of the holy angels, who, presiding over human virtue, **commands the nations.**

If you notice, the books may be talking about another man than Christ, because even Christ speaks to this man. The primary person is most likely Michael, who is Michael as a man. I she one who writes or reads? Is the man in Revelation 1:3 Michael if Christ appears to speak of him?

"Blessed is he that readeth, and they that hear the words of this prophecy, and keep those things which are written therein: for the time is at hand."
Revelation 1:3 KJV

"To him that overcometh will I grant to sit with me in my throne, even as I also overcame, and am set down with my Father in his throne."
Revelation 3:21 KJV

WHO IS HE THAT READETH?

Secret of Enoch 48

8 Blessed is the man who shall bear their yoke and shall drag them along, for he shall be released on the day of the great judgement.

"Blessed is he that readeth, and they that hear the words of this prophecy, and keep those things which are written therein: for the time is at hand."
Revelation 1:3 KJV

Who is the man that reads the books?

Enoch 58
The holy Michael, another holy angel, one of the holy ones, was sent, who raised me up.

Notice Enoch 58 says Michael is sent, but Michael is sent until the second coming or until after the Eighth Day hasn't happened yet.

Enoch 58

There I beheld the Ancient of days, whose head was like white wool, and with him another, whose countenance resembled that of man. His countenance was full of grace, like that of one of the holy angels. Then I inquired of one of the angels, who went with me, and who showed me every secret thing, concerning this son of man; who he was; whence he was; and why he accompanied the Ancient of days.

2 And when he raised me, my spirit returned; for I was incapable of enduring this vision of violence, its agitation, and the concussion of heaven.

3 Then holy Michael said to me, wherefore art thou disturbed at this vision? and he has been merciful and longsuffering towards all who dwell upon the earth.

What is the Day of Mercy? And look, Michael says man is his ancestor? But many won't see this as a man who is born after the flood, being sent back before the flood.

Enoch 58

8 And a male monster, whose name is Behemoth, which possesses, moving on his breast, the invisible wilderness.

9 His name was Dendayen in the east of the garden, where the elect and the righteous will dwell; where he received it from my ancestor, who was man, from Adam the first of men, whom the Lord of spirits made.

And those at the time of Christ saw the future. So, Christ the first fruit could be raised early. But up to now, the resurrection hasn't happened.

"But in those days, after that tribulation, the sun shall be darkened, and the moon shall not give her light,"
Mark 13:24 KJV

"**And then shall he send his angels** and shall gather together his elect from the four winds, from the uttermost part of the earth to the uttermost part of heaven."
Mark 13:27 KJV

Now once again, Michael says he was sent back in time. They are talking the eighth day which they saw, because time got stuck together. And Christ is saying that he won't send the angels until the second coming which is in our future. But yet they have already been sent, which is evidence of time travel from our future.

Enoch 58

2 And when he raised me, my spirit returned; for I was incapable of enduring this vision of violence, its agitation, and the concussion of heaven.
3 Then holy Michael said to me, wherefore art thou disturbed at this vision?
4 Hitherto has existed the day of mercy; and he has been merciful and longsuffering towards all who dwell upon the earth.

What is the Day of Mercy? Well from what I can determine, this is the period before judgment, and the plagues are released in full upon the earth. Before the storms and fire which because of more oxygen burns and can't be put out. Because of great storms seven times more powerful, and lightning seven times more intense.

Enoch 49

3 Others shall be made to see, that they must repent, and forsake the works of their hands; and that glory awaits them not in the presence of the Lord of spirits; yet that by his name they may be saved. The Lord of spirits will have compassion on them: for great is his mercy; and righteousness is in his judgment, and in the presence of his glory; nor in his judgment shall iniquity stand. He who repents not before him shall perish.

So, this sounds like before him means, if in your present life you repent. After you are raised from the dead, he will have mercy on those who have repented.

So, Michael is telling Enoch where he comes from, what period. He comes from after the judgement. If we see him walking around in white, and after the resurrection when they are clothed in white after judgment I suppose.

And those at the time of Christ saw the future. So, Christ the first fruit could be raised early. But up to now, the resurrection hasn't happened. But also said he would take up Adam, so Christ raised Adam according to the prophecy of five thousand five hundred years.

"But in those days, after that tribulation, the sun shall be darkened, and the moon shall not give her light,"
Mark 13:24 KJV

"And then shall he send his angels and shall gather together his elect from the four winds, from the uttermost part of the earth to the uttermost part of heaven."
Mark 13:27 KJV

Now once again, Michael says he was sent back in time. They are talking about the eighth day which they saw when Christ was raised, because time was stuck together then. Also, how they are not sent back until Time gets stuck together or until the end. But because time failed the end could be the beginning.

But Christ is saying he won't send his angels until the future. So, Michael the ancestor of Adam is sent back, from a future, which hasn't yet happened. But it's a period in the future which hasn't yet come

Nicodemus 14
2 Declare to your sons, the patriarchs and prophets, all those things, which thou didst hear from Michael, the archangel, when I sent thee to the gates of Paradise, to entreat God that he would anoint my head when I was sick.
3 Then Seth, coming near to the patriarchs and prophets, said, I Seth, when I was praying to God at the gates of Paradise, beheld the angel of the Lord, Michael appear unto me saying, I am sent unto thee from the Lord; I am appointed to preside over human bodies.

Nicodemus 20 (resurrection God took up Adam)

Time stuck together many taken. Yet none would happen until after the eight day, which hasn't come yet.

Nicodemus 20

THEN the Lord holding Adam by the hand, delivered him to Michael the archangel; and he led them into Paradise, filled with mercy and glory.

Nicodemus 21

4 The archangel Michael farther commanded us to go beyond Jordan, to an excellent and fat country, where there are many who rose from the dead along with us for the proof of the resurrection of Christ.

Nicodemus 22

11 And we found in the first of the seventy books, where Michael the archangel is speaking to the third son of Adam the first man, an account that after five thousand five hundred years, Christ the most beloved Son of God was come on earth,

Hermas 8 (resurrection)

25 The great and venerable angel which you saw, was Michael, who has the power over his people, and governs them. For he has planted the law in the hearts of those who have believed; and therefore, he visits them to whom he has given the law, to see if they have kept it.

The Second Book of Hermas Commands

WHEN I had prayed at home, and was sat down upon the bed, a certain man came in to me with a reverend look, in the habit of a shepherd, clothed with a white cloak, having his bag upon his back, and his staff in his hand, and saluted me.

"At the same time came the disciples unto Jesus, saying, Who is the greatest in the kingdom of heaven? And Jesus called a little child unto him, and set him in the midst of them, and said, Verily

I say unto you, except ye be converted, and become as little children, ye shall not enter into the kingdom of heaven."

Matthew 18:1-3 KJV

(31 partial) And showeth mercy to hundreds and thousands and to all that love Him.

"Blessed and holy is he that hath part in the first resurrection: on such the second death hath no power, but they shall be priests of God and of Christ and shall reign with him a thousand years."

Revelation 20:6 KJV

Enoch 58

3 Then holy Michael said to me, wherefore art thou disturbed at this vision?

4 Hitherto has existed the day of mercy; and he has been merciful and long suffering towards all who dwell upon the earth.

So, clearly Michael says he comes from the period of time after the day of mercy.

9 His name was Dendayen in the east of the garden, where the elect and the righteous will dwell; where he received it from my ancestor, who was man, from Adam the first of men, whom the Lord of spirits made.

But this sounds more like Michael the Archangel rather than Christ. Who do you know in the Bible who comes from the North seeing most all are in the navel of the earth. Further these things happen after the resurrection.

"I have raised up one from the north, and he shall come: from the rising of the sun shall he call upon my name: and he shall come upon princes as upon morter, and as the potter treadeth clay. Who hath declared from the beginning, that we may know? and beforetime, that we may say, He is righteous? yea, there is none that sheweth, yea, there is none that declareth, yea, there is none that heareth your words."

Isaiah 41:25-26 KJV

"And he that overcometh, and keepeth my works unto the end, to him will I give power over the nations: And he shall rule them with a rod of iron; as the vessels of a potter shall they be broken to shivers: even as I received of my Father."
Revelation 2:26-27 KJV

Enoch 20
5 Michael, one of the holy angels, who, presiding over human virtue, commands the nations.

You see Revelation 2: 27 even as I received of my Father. And that's Christ talking about another man than himself. And who is this man written about from before the flood who is not Christ. And whom Christ himself also speaks?

"To him that overcometh will I grant to sit with me in my throne, even as I also overcame, and am set down with my Father in his throne."
Revelation 3:21 KJV

"And he that overcometh, and keepeth my works unto the end, to him will I give power over the nations:"
Revelation 2:26 KJV

2 I returned his salutation, and immediately he sat down by me, and said unto me, I am sent by that venerable messenger, that I should dwell with thee all the remaining days of thy life.

Michael sent back in Time to Adam after was cast out of the garden. This was through fasting and prayer that God communicated Adam. This was the beginning of the teachings of the prophets and of telepathy. Adam and Eve 29:6 **And God looked upon Adam's thought,** you see that's telepathy.

Adam and Eve 8

2 Then God the Lord said unto Adam, "When thou wast under subjection to Me, thou hadst a bright nature within thee, and for that reason couldst thou see things afar off. But after thy transgression thy bright nature was withdrawn from thee; and it was not left to thee to see things afar off, but only near at hand; after the ability of the flesh; for it is brutish."

So, you see Adam was Telepathic but had his abilities taken away. But by fasting and prayer he was able again make contact God this becomes the teaching of Telepathy. You notice Moses and Christ also fasted and Christ was Telepathic? Noah also is Telepathic.

1st Book of Adam and Eve 29

6 And God looked upon Adam's thought and sent the angel Michael as far as the sea that reaches unto India, to take from thence golden rods and bring them to Adam.
7 This did God in His wisdom, in order that these golden rods, being with Adam in the cave, should shine forth with light in the night around him, and put an end to his fear of the darkness.
8 Then the angel Michael went down by God's order, took golden rods, as God had commanded him, and brought them to God.

But Christ is saying he won't send his angels until in the future. So, Michael the ancestor of Adam is sent back from a future which hasn't yet happened yet, it's a period in the future which hasn't yet come

Nicodemus 14

2 Declare to your sons, the patriarchs and prophets, all those things, which thou didst hear from Michael, the archangel, when I sent thee to the gates of Paradise, to entreat God that he would anoint my head when I was sick.
3 Then Seth, coming near to the patriarchs and prophets, said, I Seth, when I was praying to God at the gates of Paradise, beheld the angel of the Lord, Michael appears unto me saying, I am sent unto thee from the Lord; I am appointed to preside over human bodies.

Enoch Chapter 46

So, this is the man raised in the seventh millennium, and sent back in time to die a second time to save our souls in Enoch 46:1? Recall that's Christ raised in the eighth day and sent back in time to be Christ born of Mary? So, is this the second time he appeared Hebrews 9:26-28.

"For then must he often have suffered since the foundation of the world: but now once in the end of the world hath he appeared to put away sin by the sacrifice of himself. And as it is appointed unto men once to die, but after this the judgment:
Christ was once offered to bear the sins of many; and unto them that look for him shall he appear the second time without sin unto salvation."
Hebrews 9:26-28 KJV

Barnabas 13:9 and 10 Christ is raised in the eighth day. As a matter of fact, most everyone is. But due to time being stuck together those things have happened, that have not yet happened

Barnabas 13 9 (partial)
begin the eighth day, that is, the beginning of the other world.
10 For which cause we observe the eighth day with gladness, in which Jesus rose from the dead; and having manifested himself to his disciples, ascended into heaven.

The secrets of Enoch 33
AND I appointed the eighth day also, that the eighth day should be the first-created after my work, and that the first seven revolve in the form of the seventh thousand, and that at the beginning of the eighth thousand there should be a time of not-counting, endless, with neither years nor months nor weeks nor days nor hours.

The eighth day is a period when time travel is established on earth. It's also a period when I believe seven millennium are stuck together from the past earth's history this makes a new period without time. Seven millennium becoming like a single day in which all who lived in that period lives again.

Secrets of Enoch 65

5 When all creation visible and invisible, as the Lord created it, shall end, then every man goes to the great judgement, and then all-time shall perish, and the years, and thenceforward there will be neither months nor days nor hours, they will be stuck together and will not be counted.

Now looking at Secrets of Enoch 65, we see the Aeon is Time Stuck Together, also means Time Travel which is part of the mystery of God which is partly why God is God. So, if there is the father, this is the ability Christ was given by him, among other things.
And I am pretty sure Michael is one of these as are the seven angels. As for to sup, well, depend on if you are real or a vision. Does it mean resurrected of found living?

"Behold, I stand at the door, and knock: if any man hears my voice, and open the door, I will come in to him, and will sup with him, and he with me. To him that overcometh will I grant to sit with me in my throne, even as I also overcame, and am set down with my Father in his throne. He that hath an ear, let him hear what the Spirit saith unto the churches."
Revelation 3:20-22 KJV

EPIGRAPH

Formula Time Travel, Terraforming Rendition of what being talked about.

Resurrection
What I see is God taking 1000 years, and God terraforming the earth.
- divided by 7 to thin out the atmosphere
- 7 thinned out atmospheres 142.8571428571429 years, multiply 142.8571428571429 years multiplied times 7 x 7 = 7000 years of thinned out atmospheres each atmosphere 1000 years measure in time Time.

This is why these angels in Revelation these angels are holding back the four winds, "Time is Stuck Together" the atmosphere is deadly, prophetic events transacting on the earth.

"And after these things I saw four angels standing on the four corners of the earth, holding the four winds of the earth, that the wind should not blow on the earth, nor on the sea, nor on any tree."
Revelation 7:1 KJV

Resurrection 8000 or 7 millennium equal 8000 years divided (8000 divided by 8 x 7 = 56 so 8000 divided by 56 = 142.8571428571429 years x 7 = 1000 years or the 8th day Time Stuck together)

CHAPTER 5
SUPOSITION OF CHRIST

I've come to some calculation of Christ, before he came to the time of Christ two thousand years ago. I believe we have enough evidence to show he was someone else before coming. Let's look at Hebrews 9:28 again, it's saying he to appear a second time.

Fact is because time was stuck together, they saw him the second time after his resurrection which happened about two thousand to twenty-five hundred years later. And the man they saw at the resurrection is a different man than they knew.

(Partial verse) And unto them that look for him shall he appear the second time without sin unto salvation."
Hebrews 9:28 KJV

So, this is probably the real Christ who was sent back in time to be Christ.

"After that he appeared in **another form** unto two of them, as they walked, and went into the country."
Mark 16:12 KJV

This should be understood as to how the son of David could be Christ. Now, the Giants are children of the fallen angels. But David's son is much like those angels when he gets resurrected at the end.

Point he would not be able to have children coming from heaven. So those who speak of such things as if Christ was having sex and children: Why didn't we have giants on the earth after that. Like Noah also I believed to have been resurrected and sent back.

Enoch 15:8

8 Now the giants, who have been born of spirit and of flesh, shall be called upon earth evil spirits, and on earth shall be their habitation. Evil spirits shall proceed from their flesh, because they were created from above; from the holy Watchers was their beginning and primary foundation. Evil spirits shall they be upon earth, and the spirits of the wicked shall they be called. The habitation of the spirits of heaven shall be in heaven; but upon earth shall be the habitation of terrestrial spirits, who are born on earth.

EVIDENCE OF ZERO TIME

Protevangelion 13

AND leaving her and his sons in the cave, Joseph went forth to seek a Hebrew midwife in the village of Bethlehem.

2 But as I was going (said Joseph) I looked up into the air, and I saw the clouds astonished, and the fowls of the air stopping in the midst of their flight.

3 And I looked down towards the earth, and saw a table spread, and working people sitting around it, but their hands were upon the table, and they did not move to eat.

4 They who had meat in their mouths did not eat.

5 They who lifted their hands up to their heads did not draw them back:

6 And they who lifted them up to their mouths did not put anything in;

7 But all their faces were fixed upwards.

8 And I beheld the sheep dispersed, and yet the sheep stood still.

9 And the shepherd lifted up his hand to smite them, and his hand continued up.

10. And I looked unto a river and saw the kids with their mouths close to the water, and touching it, but they did not drink.

Protevangelion 14

10 Then a bright cloud overshadowed the cave, and the midwife

said, This day my soul is magnified, for mine eyes have seen surprising things, and salvation is brought forth to Israel.

11 But on a sudden the cloud became a great light in the cave, so that their eyes could not bear it.

12 But the light gradually decreased, until the infant appeared, and sucked the breast of his mother Mary.

"And to have power to heal sicknesses, and to cast out devils:"
Mark 3:15 KJV

"But if I cast out devils by the Spirit of God, then the kingdom of God is come unto you."
Matthew 12:28 KJV

Now, Christ came and showed you that we as flesh could be possessed by spirits, proving spirits can be put in us, or get out of us.

"But when the morning was now come, Jesus stood on the shore.

There are two factors here which point to the fact Christ is the son of David and brother of Solomon who is calmly black. But then after being resurrected, he's sent back in time.

"And Adonijah the son of Haggith came to Bath-sheba the mother of Solomon. And she said, comest thou peaceably? And he said, peaceably."
1 Kings 2:13 KJV

"And he that sat was to look upon like a jasper and a sardine stone: and there was a rainbow round about the throne, in sight like unto an emerald."
Revelation 4:3 KJV

"I am black, but comely, O ye daughters of Jerusalem, As the tents of Kedar, As the curtains of Solomon."
Song of Solomon 1:5 KJV

This child I believe to be Christ, or after Christ in the 8th day, another is raised and like Christ this person or person of Revelation 3:22

To him that overcometh will I grant to sit with me in my throne, even as I also overcame, and am set down with my father in his throne. He that hath an ear, let him hear what the Spirit saith unto the churches.
Revelation 3:20-22 KJV

"And it came to pass on the seventh day, that the child died. And the servants of David feared to tell him that the child was dead: for they said, Behold, while the child was yet alive, we spake unto him, and he would not hearken unto our voice: how will he then vex himself, if we tell him that the child is dead?"
2 Samuel 12:18 KJV

This man with the ancient of days is that boy grown up after the resurrection. Seeing him at the time of Enoch, we know he had not yet come to earth as a man. So the child lived only 7 days in total, that should be known.

Enoch 46:1
1 There I beheld the Ancient of days, whose head was like white wool, and with him another, whose countenance resembled that of man. His countenance was full of grace, like that of one of the holy angels. Then I inquired of one of the angels, who went with me, and who showed me every secret thing, concerning this Son of man; who he was; whence he was; and why he accompanied the Ancient of days.

He is most likely light skinned black, like his brother Solomon. But Mary's birth of him changed his appearance.

"So, Christ was once offered to bear the sins of many; and unto them that look for him shall he appear the second time without sin unto salvation."
Hebrews 9:28 KJV

The second death did not hurt him, and this was his second death.

"Now the birth of Jesus Christ was on this wise: When as his mother Mary was espoused to Joseph, before they came together, she was found with child of the Holy Ghost."
Matthew 1:18 KJV

The Protevangelion 9:13

13 But the angel returned answer, not so, O Mary, but the Holy Ghost shall come upon thee, and the power of the Most High shall overshadow thee;

"And Jesus answered and said, while he taught in the temple, how say the scribes that Christ is the son of David? For David himself said by the Holy Ghost, The LORD said to my Lord, sit thou on my right hand, Till I make thine enemies thy footstool. David therefore himself calleth him Lord; and whence is he then his son? And the common people heard him gladly."
Mark 12:35-37 KJV

So, Jesus himself speaks saying that David said by the Holy Ghost? I somehow feel there are perhaps two. I've studied and found both Christ and the father are self-eternal. It's hard to understand, how when all things vanish and there is still two yet only one created all things. But if they are both self-eternal, they wouldn't either one would require to be created.

I suppose that's the closest answer to that problem which is a time travel solution problem I could not really solve. Leading me to believe there is yet another to be raised in the eighth day, since Christ is already taken.

"After that he appeared in another form unto two of them, as they walked, and went into the country."
Mark 16:12 KJV

"But when the morning was now come, Jesus stood on the shore: but the disciples knew not that it was Jesus. This is now the third time that Jesus shewed himself to his disciples, after that he was risen from the dead."
John 21:4, 14 KJV

And when he had spoken these things, while they beheld, he was taken up; and a cloud received him out of their sight. And while they looked steadfastly toward heaven as he went up, behold, two men stood by them in white apparel; which also said, Ye men of Galilee, why stand ye gazing

up into heaven? this same Jesus, which is taken up from you into heaven, shall so come in like manner as ye have seen him go into heaven."
Acts 1:7-11 KJV

So, he no longer looked like Mary's son but looked like his former self perhaps. If not, it's another unknown man who's Christ son, perhaps if Christ is on the throne?

I guess the first place is with me, my story and why I'm doing The Sevenfold doctrine of The Whole creation. What that is, is a teaching which is prophesied to come into existence in the latter part of the seventh millennium.

We are currently in the latter part of the seventh millennium and I'm attempting to start this teaching according to this prophecy. Here, look at Daniel 12:4, its saying we dont understand until the end!

"But thou, O Daniel, shut up the words, and seal the book, even to the time of the end: many shall run to and fro, and knowledge shall be increased."
Daniel 12:4 KJV

Well, here's the thing, if we couldn't understand until the end, how did those who removed all the books of God understand what they were doing? If they did not actually understand or know what they were doing? It does say knowledge will be increased.

The reason I say that is in many cases the things the early church removed in fact the very things you need to understand what would be understanding in the last day. Looking at the Book of Enoch chapter 92, we see the teaching Daniel speaks of.

12 Afterwards, in the seventh week, a perverse generation shall arise; abundant shall be its deeds, and all its deeds perverse. During its completion, the righteous shall be selected from the everlasting plant of righteousness; and to them shall be given the sevenfold doctrine of his whole creation.

Looking at the last line, we see the title of my book and what it might imply. "The Sevenfold Doctrine" I believe a teaching of resurrection, time travel, telepathy, a moneyless system and the second coming of Christ and his angels. So, these are some of the things we will try and understand.

In this case, the seventh week is the seventh millennium from the time Adam was placed in the garden and God and cast him out into the earth he and his wife Eve. This teaching concerns the end and where God comes from and how once in power, jumped back in time, and created the heavens and the earth that we see today.

Gods coming from the future, going back before all things are created, and erased reality also started all over again.

The study looks at things which when you go back before things are created. Those in the future perhaps reverse engineer as you go back in time then things cease to exist fading from reality. But in that form are contained in the throne, with a possibility even the invisible body of the physical is also made.

Enoch 24

Lord, and the Lord spoke to me: Enoch, beloved, all thou seest, all things that are standing finished I tell thee even before the very beginning, all that I created from non-being, and visible things from invisible.

3 Hear, Enoch, and take in these my words, for not to My angels have I told my secret, and I have not told them their rise, nor my endless realm, nor have they understood my creating, which I tell thee to-day.

4 For before all things were visible, I alone used to go about in the invisible things, like the sun from east to west, and from west to east.

thing

/THiNG/

Learn to pronounce

noun

plural noun: things

1. an object that one need not, cannot, or does not wish to give a specific name to.
2. an inanimate material object as distinct from a living sentient being.

"For by him were all things created, that are in heaven, and that are in earth, visible and invisible, whether they be thrones, or dominions, or principalities, or powers: all things were created by him, and for him:"
Colossians 1:16 KJV

So, nothing existed in spirit or invisible form after Christ jumped back in time to create all things. If you jump back before all things are created, they will vanish from existence. So, if we go back to the beginning when Christ becomes God.

"Who is the image of the invisible God, the firstborn of every creature for by him were all things created, that are in heaven, and that are in earth, visible and invisible, whether they be thrones, or dominions, or principalities, or powers: all things were created by him, and for him:"
Colossians 1:15-16: KJV

"And to make all men see what is the fellowship of the mystery, which from the beginning of the world hath been hid in God, who created all things by Jesus Christ:"
Ephesians 3:9 KJV

The first born is the first resurrected. What books are saying Christ is the first resurrected among men. When he comes to power he also goes back in time and creates all things! possible Christ was raised as someone else in the "Eighth Day", if not the resurrected son of David.

The "Eighth Day" is a period when time is stuck together. During which time there is time travel back or forward in time. So, those coming may be quite advanced in technology capable of traveling to distant futures where all things have been learned or accomplished.

Time Stuck together is what will raise the dead that's if you take the seven millennium in which man has been on earth then stick all seven millennium together, all the dead in all seven millennium would be raised from the dead.

This person below in Levi 5 is possibly Christ, or a man raised who goes whom we don't know. Perhaps, a man we don't know who is sent back to be Christ. Why would I say that? Remember when Christ gets raised and the Apostles can't recognize him? It's my belief Christ is a different person than the person they all knew.

Levi 5

11 And in the seventh week shall become priests, who are idolaters, adulterers, lovers of money, proud, lawless, lascivious, abusers of children and beasts.

12 And after their punishment shall have come from the Lord, the priesthood shall fail.

13 Then shall the Lord raise up a new priest.

14 And to him all the words of the Lord shall be revealed; and he shall execute a righteous judgement upon the earth for a multitude of days.

15 And his star shall arise in heaven as of a king.

Here this is the person the Apostles did not know. Or perhaps a man who gets resurrected in the eighth day and sent back to be Christ who Enoch described. But it appears this is not Christ true appearance!

Enoch Chapter 46

There I beheld the Ancient of days, whose head was like white wool, and with him another, whose countenance resembled that of man. His countenance was full of grace, like that of one of the holy angels. Then I inquired of one of the angels, who went with me, and who showed me every secret thing, concerning this Son of man; who he was; whence he was; and why he accompanied the Ancient of days.

So, this is the man raised in the seventh millennium and sent back in time to die a second time to save our souls in Enoch 46:1? Recall Christ is raised in the eighth day and sent back in time to be Christ born of Mary? So, is this the second time he appeared Hebrews 9:26-28.

"For then must he often have suffered since the foundation of the world: but now once in the end of the world hath he appeared to put away sin by the sacrifice of himself. And as it is appointed unto men once to die, but after this the judgment: so Christ was once offered to bear the sins of many; and unto them that look for him shall he appear the second time without sin unto salvation." Hebrews 9:26-28 KJV

Barnabas 13:9 and 10 Christ is raised in the eighth day which has not yet come. But this is the meaning of what was, what is, and what is to come is how you begin to speak talking like this. I am the first and last. Time jump, perhaps when all things vanished when Christ jumped back in time to create all things. Christ was the last one to fade from existence and the first one to b e recreated in the time jump of the new creation. But that's why its what was, what is, and what is to come.

Barnabas 13 9 (partial)
begin the eighth day, that is, the beginning of the other world.
10 For which cause we observe the eighth day with gladness, in which Jesus rose from the dead; and having manifested himself to his disciples, ascended into heaven.

The secrets of Enoch 33
AND I appointed the eighth day also, that the eighth day should be the first-created after my work, and that the first seven revolve in the form of the seventh thousand, and that at the beginning of the eighth thousand there should be a time of not-counting, endless, with neither years nor months nor weeks nor days nor hours.

The eighth day is a period when time travel is established on earth. It's also a period when I believe seven millennium are stuck together from the past earth's history. To make a new period, without time. Or seven millennium are like as single day, in which the dead are raised.

Secrets of Enoch 65

5 When all creation visible and invisible, as the Lord created it, shall end, then every man goes to the great judgement, and then all-time shall perish, and the years, and thenceforward there will be neither months nor days nor hours, they will be stuck together and will not be counted.

Now looking at Secrets of Enoch 65, we see the Aeon is Time Stuck Together, it also means Time Travel which actually is part of the mystery of God which is partly why God is God. So, if there is the father, this is the ability Christ was given by him, among other things.

Enoch 15:8

Here we see Christ is proving that these spirits are here which he cast out. This is their origin. Christ showing evidence of these spirits are remnant of the fallen angels their children.

8 Now the giants, who have been born of spirit and of flesh, shall be called upon earth evil spirits, and on earth shall be their habitation. Evil spirits shall proceed from their flesh, because they were created from above; from the holy Watchers was their beginning and primary foundation. Evil spirits shall they be upon earth, and the spirits of the wicked shall they be called. The habitation of the spirits of heaven shall be in heaven; but upon earth shall be the habitation of terrestrial spirits, who are born on earth.

"And to have power to heal sicknesses, and to cast out devils:"
Mark 3:15 KJV

THESE ARE THOUGHT RELATED ISSUES RELATED TO FOREIGN THOUGHT

"But if I cast out devils by the Spirit of God, then the kingdom of God is come unto you."
Matthew 12:28 KJV

"And he asked him, what is thy name? And he answered, saying, my name is Legion: for we are many. And he besought him much that he would not send them away out of the country. Now there was there nigh unto the mountains a great herd of swine feeding. And all the devils besought him, saying, send us into the swine, that we may enter into them. And forthwith Jesus gave them leave. And the unclean spirits went out and entered into the swine: and the herd ran violently down a steep place into the sea, (they were about two thousand;) and were choked in the sea. And they that fed the swine fled, and told it in the city, and in the country. And they went out to see what it was that was done."
Mark 5:9-14 KJV

Question, how can understanding that thought you transmitted one to another hurt or help the system? Question how can those who reject the transference of thought, change their ways if they are proven wrong? When they think all thought generated within themselves are of themselves. Yet, they have peer pressure, and low esteem, and people who try and make you look wrong by causing others to turn against you. Why is it so important others feel, think and act like you?

"But Peter and they that were with him were heavy with sleep: and when they were awake, they saw his glory, and the two men that stood with him. And it came to pass, as they departed from him, Peter said unto Jesus, Master, it is good for us to be here: and let us make three tabernacles; one for thee, and one for Moses, and one for Elias: not knowing what he said. While he thus spake, there came a cloud, and overshadowed them: and they feared as they entered into the cloud. And there came a voice out of the cloud, saying, This is my beloved Son: hear him. And when the voice was past, Jesus was found alone. And they kept it close, and told no man in those days any of those things which they had seen."
Luke 9:32-36 KJV

"And was transfigured before them: and his face did shine as the sun, and his raiment was white as the light. And, behold, there appeared unto them Moses and Elias talking with him. Then answered Peter, and said unto Jesus, Lord, it is good for us to be here: if thou wilt, let us make here three tabernacles; one for thee, and one for Moses, and one for Elias. While he yet spake, behold, a bright cloud overshadowed them: and behold a voice out of the cloud, which said, This

is my beloved Son, in whom I am well pleased; hear ye him. And when the disciples heard it, they fell on their face, and were sore afraid. And Jesus came and touched them, and said, Arise, and be not afraid. And when they had lifted up their eyes, they saw no man, save Jesus only. And as they came down from the mountain, Jesus charged them, saying, Tell the vision to no man, until the Son of man be risen again from the dead."
Matthew 17:2-9 KJV

"And his raiment became shining, exceeding white as snow; so as no fuller on earth can white them. And there appeared unto them Elias with Moses: and they were talking with Jesus. And Peter answered and said to Jesus, Master, it is good for us to be here: and let us make three tabernacles; one for thee, and one for Moses, and one for Elias. For he wist not what to say; for they were sore afraid. And there was a cloud that overshadowed them: and a voice came out of the cloud, saying, this is my beloved Son: hear him. And suddenly, when they had looked round about, they saw no man anymore, save Jesus only with themselves. And as they came down from the mountain, he charged them that they should tell no man what things they had seen, till the son of man were risen from the dead.
Mark 9:3-9 KJV

And Christ was quite specific about not talking about this until after the resurrection. See, this is proving they are already resurrected and they are all coming from the future. They are coming from a resurrection which doesn't happen for 480 years more or less.

EPIGRAPH

Resurrection Theory

- if the dead are "Raised in A Linear Way" all born in the first 142.8571428571429 years of each of the 7 millennium. Should be the first then of those born in newly created 1000-year period or 8th Day. The second 142.8571428571429 years of all seven millennium are those raised from the dead born in that period perhaps. And those born the same time per 1000-year period, so on and so forth, almost to the end of the eighth day. But the resurrection would be required to be sped up, or they come earlier in the seventh millennium to fight and overcome before the end of the thousand-year period. It's also prophecy for use to judge the angels even us as angels. So, if they come earlier at the end of the seventh millennium to have a 1000 years peace until the end of 8th millennium and still have time to fight at Armageddon before the end of the eight millennium.

This time travel formula could not work on a flat surface but works better on an orb. Because all people being raised occupy the same time and space, yet at different times which get stuck together. The same coordinates, so God foresaw the orb as the best design to support Time Travel.

CHAPTER 6
REBORN

POSSIBILITY THESE CHILDREN MAY HAVE BEEN REINSURTED (BORN AGAIN)

Is there a possibility that after resurrection they have replanted a man soul in a body newly born. In a time before the resurrection? A soul learned and taught.

"Howbeit, because by this deed thou hast given great occasion to the enemies of the LORD to blaspheme, the child also that is born unto thee shall surely die. And Nathan departed unto his house. And the LORD struck the child that Uriah's wife bare unto David, and it was very sick. David therefore besought God for the child; and David fasted, and went in, and lay all night upon the earth. And the elders of his house arose, and went to him, to raise him up from the earth: but he would not, neither did he eat bread with them. And it came to pass on the seventh day, that the child died. And the servants of David feared to tell him that the child was dead: for they said, Behold, while the child was yet alive, we spake unto him, and he would not hearken unto our voice: how will he then vex himself, if we tell him that the child is dead? But when David saw that his servants whispered, David perceived that the child was dead: therefore David said unto his servants, Is the child dead? And they said, He is dead."
2 Samuel 12:14-19 KJV

This is evidence time was stopped at the birth of Christ or evidence where this ship came from was a place with no time. So, coming into the physical time is stop at the portal or opening or the place the heaven open and something passed through the opening.

Enoch 105
1 After a time, my son Mathusala took a wife for his son Lamech.
2 She became pregnant by him, and brought forth a child, the flesh of which was as white as snow, and red as a rose; the hair of whose head was white like wool, and long; and whose eyes were

beautiful. When he opened them, he illuminated all the house, like the sun; the whole house abounded with light.

3 And when he was taken from the hand of the midwife, opening also his mouth, he spoke to the Lord of righteousness. Then Lamech his father was afraid of him; and flying away came to his own father Mathusala, and said, I have begotten a son, unlike to other children. He is not human; but, resembling the offspring of the angels of heaven, is of a different nature from ours, being altogether unlike to us.

4 His eyes are bright as the rays of the sun; his countenance glorious, and he looks not as if he belonged to me, but to the angels.

14 A great destruction therefore shall come upon all the earth; a deluge, a great destruction, shall take place in one year.

15 This child which is born to you shall survive on the earth, and his three sons shall be saved with him. When all mankind who are on earth shall die, he shall be safe.

16 And his posterity shall beget on the earth giants, not spiritual, but carnal. Upon the earth shall a great punishment be inflicted, and it shall be washed from all corruption. Now therefore inform thy son Lamech, that he who is born is his child in truth; and he shall call his name Noah, for he shall be to you a survivor.

Jasher 2

23 And in the end of days and years, when Zillah became old, the Lord opened her womb.

24 And she conceived and bare a son and she called his name Tubal Cain, saying, After I had withered away have I obtained him from the Almighty God.

25 And she conceived again and bare a daughter, and she called her name Naamah, for she said, After I had withered away have, I obtained pleasure and delight.

26 And Lamech was old and advanced in years, and his eyes were dim that he could not see, and Tubal Cain, his son, was leading him and it was one day that Lamech went into the field and Tubal Cain his son was with him, and whilst they were walking in the field, Cain the son of Adam advanced towards them; for Lamech was very old and could not see much, and Tubal Cain his son was very young.

27 And Tubal Cain told his father to draw his bow, and with the arrows he smote Cain, who was yet far off, and he slew him, for he appeared to them to be an animal.

28 And the arrows entered Cain's body although he was distant from them, and he fell to the ground and died.

29 And the Lord requited Cain's evil according to his wickedness, which he had done to his brother Abel, according to the word of the Lord which he had spoken.

30 And it came to pass when Cain had died, that Lamech and Tubal went to see the animal which they had slain, and they saw, and behold Cain their grandfather was fallen dead upon the earth.

31 And Lamech was very much grieved at having done this, and in clapping his hands together he struck his son and caused his death.

So according to this, if Christ had, had children they would have been giants on the earth after that like with Noah and the fallen angels which in fact, they had giants because they are from the resurrection. Being from heaven, they as resurrected men having children being from heaven also would create Giants, like did Noah. Those giants after the flood are because of Noah which is a good reason to suggest he's like Christ. And Noah came from heaven did Christ, they just didn't tell us, accept by deductive reasoning. The only thing they told us is though was, Noah looked like an angel, but he was a man. And he was from the first resurrection. Christ is also from the resurrection born again, may be more than just words in these books.

Enoch 105

10 And now, my father, hear me; for to my son Lamech a child has been born, who resembles not him; and whose nature is not like the nature of man. His color is whiter than snow; he is redder than the rose; the hair of his head is whiter than white wool; his eyes are like the rays of the sun; and when he opened them he illuminated the whole house.

11 When also he was taken from the hand of the midwife, he opened his mouth, and blessed the Lord of heaven.

12 His father Lamech feared, and fled to me, believing not that the child belonged to him, but that he resembled the angels of heaven. And behold I am come to thee, that thou mightest point out to me the truth.

NOTE: Fact is Noah is born looking like us when we get resurrected, look at Daniels 12.

"And many of them that sleep in the dust of the earth shall awake, some to everlasting life, and some to shame and everlasting contempt. And they that be wise shall shine as the brightness of the firmament; and they that turn many to righteousness as the stars for ever and ever."
Daniel 12:2-3 KJV

Which is a sign being overlooked. Mainly because people don't take things written in the teaching seriously or those things are being misinterpreted.

14 A great destruction therefore shall come upon all the earth; a deluge, a great destruction, shall take place in one year.
15 This child which is born to you shall survive on the earth, and his three sons shall be saved with him. When all mankind who are on earth shall die, he shall be safe.
16 And his posterity shall beget on the earth giants, not spiritual, but carnal. Upon the earth shall a great punishment be inflicted, and it shall be washed from all corruption. **Now therefore inform thy son Lamech, that he who is born is his child in truth; and he shall call his name Noah,** for he shall be to you a survivor. He and his children shall be saved from the corruption which shall take place in the world; from all the sin and from all the iniquity which shall be consummated on earth in his days. Afterwards shall greater impiety take place than that which had been before consummated on the earth; for I am acquainted with holy mysteries, which the Lord himself has discovered and explained to me; and which I have read in the tablets of heaven.

EPIGRAPH

The Story of Christ is a story of a man who jumped so far back in Time, nothing existed. He left Heaven as a sign to prove he was here. Like Kilroy was here so to speak.

Colossians 1:17 is telling you Christ jumped back in time before all things.

"And he is before all things, and by him all things consist."
Colossians 1:17 KJV

Question: Time Travel is or Time Stuck together the only way a man born on earth could go back before all things. Further those clothed in white happen maybe after judgement and judgments does not happen until the throne is built. The Throne may not be built for 1500 years, and judgments after that.

be·fore
/bəˈfôr/
adverb
1.during the period of time preceding a particular event or time.

"All things were made by him; and without him was not anything made that was made."
John 1:3 KJV

Deductive Reasoning says, because of that statement in John 1:3 the planet Christ came from vanished from existence while traveling back in Time, because he's before all things.

The Solution to the problems God left us is Time, being stopped or failing, which solution also for raising the dead.

"And to make all men see what is the fellowship of the mystery, which from the beginning of the world hath been hid in God, who created all things by Jesus Christ:"
Ephesians 3:9 KJV

Time Travel back in time would cause all things to vanish. Deductive Reasoning says because time failed, they could be from a million years in the future. So, raising the dead is possible.

CHAPTER 7
TELEPATHIC CHILDREN

Now these Telepathic children may in fact be those resurrected aged and taught and sent back in time. They seem to be very intelligent at birth. The thing is if Christ had had children they most likely would have been giants based on all that's written on the matter. So again, I say, those who teach such matters about Christ can be proven wrong because we didn't have Giants born in his lineage.

So, because Tubal Cain may have been resurrected from the end and sent back in time being reborn as Noah. One clue is Giants because Noah May have been from Heaven being resurrected, he birthed giants in the earth after that.

"There were giants in the earth in those days; and also, after that, when the sons of God came in unto the daughters of men, and they bear children to them, the same became mighty men which were of old, men of renown."
Genesis 6:4 KJV

The first Gospel of Infancy
THE following accounts we found in the book of Joseph the high priest, called by some Caiaphas.
2 He relates, that Jesus spake even when he was in the cradle, and said to his mother:
3 Mary, I am Jesus the Son of God, that word which thou didst bring forth according to the declaration of the angel Gabriel to thee, and my father hath sent me for the salvation of the world.

"Howbeit, because by this deed thou hast given great occasion to the enemies of the LORD to blaspheme, the child also that is born unto thee shall surely die. And Nathan departed unto his house. And the LORD struck the child that Uriah's wife bare unto David, and it was very sick. David therefore besought God for the child; and David fasted, and went in, and lay all night upon the earth.

And the elders of his house arose, and went to him, to raise him up from the earth: but he would not, neither did he eat bread with them. And it came to pass on the seventh day, that the child died. And the servants of David feared to tell him that the child was dead: for they said, Behold, while the child was yet alive, we spake unto him, and he would not hearken unto our voice: how will he then vex himself, if we tell him that the child is dead?

But when David saw that his servants whispered, David perceived that the child was dead: therefore, David said unto his servants, Is the child dead? And they said, He is dead."
2 Samuel 12:14-19 KJV

Now if this is Tubal Cain being put in Noah, then the very reason that Christ didn't have children by the teachings of those clever people trying to bring down the name of Christ as if a normal man.

Enoch 105
1 After a time, my son Mathusala took a wife for his son Lamech.
2 She became pregnant by him, and brought forth a child, the flesh of which was as white as snow, and red as a rose; the hair of whose head was white like wool, and long; and whose eyes were beautiful. When he opened them, he illuminated all the house, like the sun; the whole house abounded with light.
3 And when he was taken from the hand of the midwife, opening also his mouth, he spoke to the Lord of righteousness. Then Lamech his father was afraid of him; and flying away came to his own father Mathusala, and said, I have begotten a son, unlike to other children. He is not human; but, resembling the offspring of the angels of heaven, is of a different nature from ours, being altogether unlike to us.
4 His eyes are bright as the rays of the sun; his countenance glorious, and he looks not as if he belonged to me, but to the angels.

"That which is born of the flesh is flesh; and that which is born of the Spirit is spirit. Marvel not that I said unto thee, Ye must be born again."
John 3:6-7 KJV

Jubilees 23

26 And in those days the children will begin to study the laws, and to seek the commandments,
And to return to the path of righteousness.

27 And the days will begin to grow many and increase amongst those children of men,
Till their days draw nigh to one thousand years,
And to a greater number of years than (before) was the number of the days.

28 And there will be no old man
Nor one who is not satisfied with his days,
For all will be (as) children and youths.

29 And all their days they will complete and live in peace and in joy, And there will be no Satan nor any evil destroyer; For all their days will be days of blessing and healing,

30 And at that time the Lord will heal His servants,
And they will rise up and see great peace, and drive out their adversaries And the righteous will see and be thankful, And rejoice with joy for ever and ever,
And will see all their judgments and all their curses on their enemies.

31 And their bones will rest in the earth, and their spirits will have much joy, they will enjoy a blessed immortality And they will know that it is the Lord who executeth judgment, And showeth mercy to hundreds and thousands and to all that love Him.

32 And do thou, Moses, write down these words; for thus are they written, and they record (them) on the heavenly tables for a testimony for the generations for ever.

"And I looked, and, lo, a Lamb stood on the mount Sion, and with him an hundred forty and four thousand, having his Father's name written in their foreheads. These are they which were not defiled with women; for they are virgins. These are they which follow the Lamb whithersoever he goeth. These were redeemed from among men, being the firstfruits unto God and to the Lamb."
Revelation 14:1, 4 KJV

I have speculated Tubal Cain was reborn as Noah and David's dead son of 7 days reborn as Christ.

The Day of Mercy; well that's also a part of the same period at the end as the scripture above in the book of Jubilees. Just confirming that thousand years when perhaps Satan is bound.

The Day of Mercy is the 1000-year period of peace at his coming, before Satan is loosed.

Jubilees 23

27 And the days will begin to grow many and increase amongst those children of men,

Till their days draw nigh to one thousand years,

30 And at that time the Lord will heal His servants,

And they will rise up and see great peace,

14 A great destruction therefore shall come upon all the earth; a deluge, a great destruction, shall take place in one year.

15 This child which is born to you shall survive on the earth, and his three sons shall be saved with him. When all mankind who are on earth shall die, he shall be safe.

16 **And his posterity shall beget on the earth giants,** not spiritual, but carnal. Upon the earth shall a great punishment be inflicted, and it shall be washed from all corruption. Now therefore inform thy son Lamech, that he who is born is his child in truth; and he shall call his name Noah, for he shall be to you a survivor.

So the giants after the flood are the result of Noah, who could have been then the resurrected son of Lamech, returned after the resurrection in the future and time travel was enacted on the earth.

Jasher 2

23 And in the end of days and years, when Zillah became old, the Lord opened her womb.

24 And she conceived and bare a son and she called his name Tubal Cain, saying, After I had withered away have I obtained him from the Almighty God.

25 And she conceived again and bare a daughter, and she called her name Naamah, for she said, After I had withered away have, I obtained pleasure and delight.

26 And Lamech was old and advanced in years, and his eyes were dim that he could not see, and Tubal Cain, his son, was leading him and it was one day that Lamech went into the field and Tubal

Cain his son was with him, and whilst they were walking in the field, Cain the son of Adam advanced towards them; for Lamech was very old and could not see much, and Tubal Cain his son was very young.

27 And Tubal Cain told his father to draw his bow, and with the arrows he smote Cain, who was yet far off, and he slew him, for he appeared to them to be an animal.

28 And the arrows entered Cain's body although he was distant from them, and he fell to the ground and died.

29 And the Lord requited Cain's evil according to his wickedness, which he had done to his brother Abel, according to the word of the Lord which he had spoken.

30 And it came to pass when Cain had died, that Lamech and Tubal went to see the animal which they had slain, and they saw, and behold Cain their grandfather was fallen dead upon the earth.

31 And Lamech was very much grieved at having done this, and in clapping his hands together he struck his son and caused his death.

Jubilees 23

26 And in those days the children will begin to study the laws, and to seek the commandments, and to return to the path of righteousness.

27 And the days will begin to grow many and increase amongst those children of men,

Till their days draw nigh to one thousand years,

And to a greater number of years than (before) was the number of the days.

28 And there will be no old man

Nor one who is not satisfied with his days,

For all will be (as) children and youths.

29 And all their days they will complete and live in peace and in joy, and there will be no Satan nor any evil destroyer; For all their days will be days of blessing and healing,

30 And at that time the Lord will heal His servants,

And they will rise up and see great peace, and drive out their adversaries and the righteous will see and be thankful, and rejoice with joy for ever and ever,

And will see all their judgments and all their curses on their enemies.

31 And their bones will rest in the earth, and their spirits will have much joy, they will enjoy a blessed immortality and they will know that it is the Lord who executeth judgment, and showeth mercy to hundreds and thousands and to all that love Him.

32 And do thou, Moses, write down these words; for thus are they written, and they record (them) on the heavenly tables for a testimony for the generations forever.

"And I heard a voice from heaven, as the voice of many waters, and as the voice of a great thunder: and I heard the voice of harpers harping with their harps: and they sung as it were a new song before the throne, and before the four beasts, and the elders: and no man could learn that song but the hundred and forty and four thousand, which were redeemed from the earth. These are they which were not defiled with women; for they are virgins. These are they which follow the Lamb whithersoever he goeth. These were redeemed from among men, being the first fruits unto God and to the Lamb."

Revelation 14:2-4 KJV

EPIGRAPH

Telepathy

So here's the thing, the same as me and my girlfriend ate of the same plater of mixed foods and thought to grab the same slice of salami while having many different salami types and slices, cheese, crackers and some veg on it. Like eating out of the same plate of French Fries, thinking to grab the same French Fry at the same time.

When you do things as one, it's easier to join as one, this is the teaching of God.
I mean, watching a TV show, you see a person walking down the hall towards a doorway. With many things going on in these frames in the foreground or background, or focusing on what weapon they might be carrying.

When you both look at the sign above the door as he walks towards it. At the same time you both focus on and read it both at the same time having one reading aloud while you read silent. But both focused on the same item in the picture with many things happening in that picture at the same time. Reading every word at the same time though reading one silent and one aloud.

You see Telepathy is almost invisible if not taught to see it even if you are the smartest man on earth, you are blinded by the teachings you believe!

CHAPTER 8
CHRISTIAN LAW / TELEPATHY

The Kingdom of Heaven – Sevenfold Doctrine of the Whole Creation

This is the teaching and the basis of the teaching; this is a requirement for anything to be taught in the church. You should have two or three, witnesses, prophets or apostles to confirm.

That any critic, must have two or three proofs against a proof to prove wrong anything in this teaching. It must not be two or three saying its wrong without proof. It must be two or three proofs of God or related to the truth of God.

THE TRUE DOCTRINE IS BASED ON TWO OR THREE

"Let the prophets speak two or three and let the other judge."
1 Corinthians 14:29 KJV

"Again, I say unto you, that if two of you shall agree on earth as touching anything that they shall ask, it shall be done for them of my Father which is in heaven. For where two or three are gathered together in my name, there am I in the midst of them."
Matthew 18:19-20 KJV

"This is the third time I am coming to you. In the mouth of two or three witnesses shall every word be established."
2 Corinthians 13:1 KJV

"But if he will not hear thee, then take with thee one or two more, that in the mouth of two or three witnesses every word may be established."
Matthew 18:16 KJV

TELEPATHY

ARCHANGELS

Note most of my studies have bordered on the teaching of Telepathy. I saw they are teaching Telepathy in the Bible and missing books in some cases. But, the teaching is being misinterpreted and being viewed as if it was any other teaching of non-Telepathic or normal people. So, its not being viewed as Telepathy, because the teaching is not being followed. The way of the government is the way people go and that's non Telepathic.

Secrets of Enoch 29
AND thence those men took me and bore me up on to the sixth heaven, and there I saw seven bands of angels, very bright and very glorious, and their faces shining more than the sun's shining, glistening, and there is no difference in their faces, or behavior, or manner of dress; and these make the orders, and learn the goings of the stars, and the alteration of the moon, or revolution of the sun, and the good government of the world.

Concepts of telepathy runs parallel with the teachings and ways of the Archangels. Funny I conceived something which is taught elsewhere in Heaven. Well studying one long ago, I began to see it as a easy way to solve problems. Turns out the Archangels themselves teach one in all things.

CONCEPTS OF TELEPATHY

So, what I have done is created a study of one, to cause people to think the same thought. For the study of Telepathy. In theory,
1- the study builds all single homes, family homes and homes of one architectural design and color. Having no difference with exact same floor plans.

2- walls can be removed to attach prefab rooms to adjust the sizes of the homes from single to family.

3- interior all exact, nothing inside different.

4- streets and cities all exact, business in the exact same place in multiple cities exactly alike.

5- so, that a worker living in a house in this city would have a coworker doing his exact same job, living in the exact same house, but in another city exactly like his city. in multiple countries which all speak different languages having one teaching with no language.

6- if every city is identical and every store shelf exactly alike. Every rule is the same, no difference from one place to another. All workers at every job, that do the same job. Could all switch places from one city to another all over the world. Could go to another country and know already where they live, work, shop without help from anyone. That's 100% of all workers in every city worldwide could switch and be at home, wherever they go.

"And the second is like unto it, thou shalt love thy neighbor as thyself."
Matthew 22:39 KJV

And this is some of what I can formulate to enhance Telepathy in the earth all having one way, one teaching and one belief and one mind.

Here's the thing when you do things as one, when you have problems.

7- you all have the same problems

8- his or her problem is no more important than your problem

9- you are of one accord and correct all problems with one solution moving to perfection.

10- Fixing one problem you might fix all problems.

It's not like your ways and beliefs, having so many problems you can't fix them. Because every person has different problems being so diverse.

You may not agree with it, but it would eliminate most of the problems created. by different strokes for different folk's world. Thing is I fasted like Adam and got Telepathy 40 days, I knew Satan was black and all these things twenty years before reading it. Not by your interpretation, but by the books of God.

Telepathy

"While Peter thought on the vision, the Spirit said unto him, Behold, three men seek thee. Arise therefore, and get thee down, and go with them, doubting nothing: for I have sent them."
Acts 10:19-20 KJV

This is Telepathy being described "See Altogether."

Esdras 6:20, 21
20 And when the world, that shall begin to vanish away, shall be finished, then will I shew these tokens: the books shall be opened before the firmament, and they shall see all together:
all together
phrase of all
all in one place or in a group; all at once

TELEPATHY STUDY

"Unto whom it was revealed, that not unto themselves, but unto us they did minister the things, which are now reported unto you by them that have preached the gospel unto you with the Holy Ghost sent down from heaven, which things the angels desire to look into."
1 Peter 1:12 KJV

So, if UFOs are angels and they come and you have Telepathy, they told you already why they came.

And if you see altogether, there probably talking about being put in a trance, having effect worldwide.

Telepathy

So, as we study telepathy and being one, in order to think the same thought. So, my girlfriend has started to adjust to my ways, hearing me complain about this or that. So, we ate, and I saw after I had rested see got seconds and another plate. While she was dressing to go to her parents for Christmas, I also got seconds and laid my plate down. She had came back and sat down.
twenty minutes to a half hour pass, I was sitting in one chair her in another. She jumped up and got her plate to take into the kitchen. But, at that same moment I was about to do the same.

I simply told her to give it to me, as I also was about to do both plates and she not. See, the thing is, I don't think she saw both plates, so she would not think to take them both, though it's Telepathy.

"Having then gifts differing according to the grace that is given to us, whether prophecy, let us prophesy according to the proportion of faith;"
Romans 12:6 KJV (in part)

"For who maketh thee to differ from another? and what hast thou that thou didst not receive? now if thou didst receive it, why dost thou glory, as if thou hadst not received it?"
1 Corinthians 4:7 KJV (in part)

Point is this, these things might affect every person differently and that may be a problem for science. Science assumes that objects and events in natural systems occur in consistent patterns that are understandable through measurement and observation. Here Nebuchadnezzar joined with beast and became one, until his hair was matted.

"let his heart be changed from man's, and let a beast's heart be given unto him; and let seven times pass over him. This matter is by the decree of the watchers, and the demand by the word of the holy ones: to the intent that the living may know that the Most High ruleth in the kingdom of men, and giveth it to whomsoever he will, and setteth up over it the basest of men."
Daniel 4:16-17 KJV (in part)

The same hour was the thing fulfilled upon Nebuchadnezzar: and he was driven from men, and did eat grass as oxen, and his body was wet with the dew of heaven, till his hairs were grown like eagles' feathers, and his nails like birds' claws."
Daniel 4:16, 33 KJV

Telepathy
Pretty common thing, small and seemingly insignificant. But when the same thing happens time and again it becomes a pattern. Doing the "Shuler King show at Cap City Comedy Club "with my girlfriend and cousin it was a good show. I ordered some food, shared some french fries with my girlfriend to save money. Now that led to this, we both thought to grab the same french fry at the same time, thinking the same thing at the same time.

Note a small thing, yet that same thing is Telepathy, but that same thing enhanced can lead to mind reading. It's not always at the level of mind reading, but it's still the same thing. God will tell you I was right on the matter; I have no fear in this. It may be called by another name, a spirit or a Holy Spirit, but the same. What I began to see was every was whenever we ate from the same plate we would think the same thought at the same time, no matter how many items are in that plate, very assorted.

So, he suffered from something which joined him with beast. I have seen Telepathy join you with things other that people. Do you think if a dog transmits a picture of something they look at is much different than a person looking at the same thing transmitting the picture.

Telepathy
Broken Transmission: My girlfriend asked me to open a can of tomato paste, she was having trouble. I picked up the tomato paste and the tomato sauce, because she wanted me to move.
So, as I am opening the paste, I'm thinking about wondering about opening the sauce. She says why did you take the sauce it's already open. Believe it are not these are Telepathic transmissions not fully developed, we are not getting the entire message and they blend with your thinking yet

thinking about the same thing in the same moment. This is the obstacle, and why we can't see Telepathy, but certain things can rise you above this stage.

Telepathy

So, here's the thing, the same as me and my girlfriend ate of the same plater of mixed foods and thought to grab the same slice of salami. With many different salami types and slices. Slices cheese, crackers and some veg on it. Like eating out of the same plate of french fries, thinking to grab the same french fry at the same time. When you do things as one, it's easier to join as one, this is the teaching of God. I mean, watching a TV show, you see a person walking down the hall towards a doorway. With many things going on in these frames. Foreground, background, what weapon they might be carrying. You both look at the sign above the door as he walks towards it. At the same time, you both focus on and read it, both at the same time. Or one reading aloud, while you read silent. But both focused on the same item in the picture, with many things happening in that picture at the same time. You see Telepathy is almost invisible if not taught to see it, even if you are the smartest man on earth, you are blinded by the teachings you believe.

Telepathy

One of my odder Telepathic events happened at work. I was working shipping receiving, running inventory stores, running handlers and other equipment on the test floor. One of the office girls came out back to smoke a cigarette. I think I was outside finishing up with FedEx at shipping and receiving. So, I stayed, stayed outside to talk with her. As I looked at her, I thought she was pregnant, yet she showed no signs of pregnancy. So, I asked; are you pregnant as she began to smoke. She said, no why do you ask? I don't think I gave her a clear answer. She later came back a couple or few weeks later saying I am pregnant. A little time after that or that time, she said. I was talking to Elf and asked her what sex my baby would be? Elf was a Berkeley psychic but told her, a girl or a boy I don't know. She said go ask Mike he's Telepathic he might know. So, this is in the first few weeks or a month of the pregnancy. I was about to say I can't do that, but my thought was interrupted by thinking to say what she wanted. And as I thought that she said a boy, but at that same time I saw a girl. I realized we had had joined as one, at the same moment, thinking the same thought at the same time, yet didn't. I told her I saw a girl; she continued saying she wanted a boy. We sat in the cafeteria with HR in there, I repeated it and why it's a girl, with witnesses there. We had to wait two or three months to find out by ultrasound. Which also said it's a girl and she later had a girl.

Telepathy At a Distance
I was backing my truck up to a client's dock, as I was bumping the dock.
A thought popped into my head that my ex-wife after a few years of separation and divorce was talking with my mother. I did not note the time, because I doubted my mom would remember that specific. But when I got home some hours later, my mom said I talked to your ex-wife today. (Here name)

Point: I did not know what they talked about, but I know it's possible to know what they talked about. God saw fit, not to give me that ability so I accept that. But I know it's possible to know more. This is the same spirit recorded in the books of God, and no man is capable of proving that wrong, by God standards.

Telepathic   Projection
Now here's something psychology can really twist the facts on. Further the perpetrator may be listening. 3am one morning doing homework, stepped outside to the curb had a cup of coffee. Sprinklers at the school going across the street, sounds muted by it. Thought I heard a sound, but maybe it's just the sprinklers brushing the trees. Suddenly I thought I saw something out the side of my eye. I jumped while turning to look and spill my coffee while it splashed. But when I turned to look, I saw nothing and no one.

But Telepathy is like radar, and puts you on remote, so my head turned automatically, and eyes focused on a tree about 50 yards away. I saw a head peering from behind that tree in the distance. Now, it was dark outside, don't forget and a person came creeping out behind a tree, and crept to the next tree. Crept from that tree to another in a line of trees, till he was just across from me. Wearing a sack over his head and eyes cut out, carrying a rifle painted white, like ROTC.

By now as he crept, I crept towards the house and front door from the sidewalk. By the time he was directly across from me he pointed his white rifle at me. I slipped into the house and called the police; I advised them they had a creeping terror on the loose. Two or three minutes later, the area was being swept with spotlights from police cars.

Telepathy

But that's Telepathic projection, like when Archie and I played chess. I saw his arm move in the side of my eye. When I turned to look, I saw the projection of his arm moving. Then I saw his arm move like the image moved. And it was exactly like I saw it.

Thing is I fasted like Adam and got Telepathy 40 days, I knew Satan was black and all these things twenty years before reading it.

Not by your interpretation, but by the books of God.

Telepathy

"While Peter thought on the vision, the Spirit said unto him, Behold, three men seek thee. Arise therefore, and get thee down, and go with them, doubting nothing: for I have sent them."
Acts 10:19-20 KJV

This is Telepathy being described "See Altogether." Now, by your interpretation of altogether you see it like at a show in which when it ends you clap altogether. And it's that viewpoint which makes it impossible to see Telepathy because you look at life a certain way. But if you not planning to talk and suddenly you begin to talk and everyone around you suddenly starts to talk saying the same thing at the same time and going into a trance where you see nothing else but what said, may as well be blind, because your so deep in thought you cant see.

Esdras 6:20, 21
20 And when the world, that shall begin to vanish away, shall be finished, then will I shew these tokens: the books shall be opened before the firmament, and they shall see all together:
all together
phrase of all
all in one place or in a group; all at once

"Unto whom it was revealed, that not unto themselves, but unto us they did minister the things, which are now reported unto you by them that have preached the gospel unto you with the Holy Ghost sent down from heaven, which things the angels desire to look into."
1 Peter 1:12 KJV

So, if UFOs are angels and they come and you have Telepathy, they told you already why they came. And if you see altogether, there probably talking about being put in a trance, having effect worldwide.
Romans 12:6 KJV (in part)

"Having then gifts differing according to the grace that is given to us, "Having then gifts differing according to the grace that is given to us, whether prophecy, let us prophesy according to the proportion of faith;"
Romans 12:6 KJV (in part)
1 Corinthians 4:7 KJV (in part)

"For who maketh thee to differ from another? and what hast thou that thou didst not receive? now if thou didst receive it, why dost thou glory, as if thou hadst not received it?"
1 Corinthians 4:7 KJV (in part)

Point is this, these things might affect every person differently and that may be a problem for science. Science assumes that objects and events in natural systems occur in consistent patterns that are understandable through measurement and observation. Here Nebuchadnezzar joined with beast and became one, until his hair was matted.

"let his heart be changed from man's, and let a beast's heart be given unto him; and let seven times pass over him. This matter is by the decree of the watchers, and the demand by the word of the holy ones: to the intent that the living may know that the Most High ruleth in the kingdom of men, and giveth it to whomsoever he will, and setteth up over it the basest of men."
Daniel 4:16-17 KJV (in part)

The same hour was the thing fulfilled upon Nebuchadnezzar: and he was driven from men, and did eat grass as oxen, and his body was wet with the dew of heaven, till his hairs were grown like eagles' feathers, and his nails like birds' claws."
Daniel 4:16, 33 KJV

So, he suffered from something which joined him with beast.

Telepathy
Broken Transmission, My girlfriend asked me to open a can of tomato paste, she was having trouble. I picked up the tomato paste and the tomato sauce, because she wanted me to move. So, as I am opening the paste, I'm thinking about wondering about opening the sauce. She says why did you take the sauce it's already open. Believe it are not these are Telepathic transmissions not fully developed, we are not getting the entire message and they blend with your thinking yet thinking about the same thing in the same moment. This is the obstacle, and why we can't see Telepathy, but certain things can rise you above this stage.

Telepathy
One of my odder Telepathic events happened at work. I was working shipping receiving, running inventory stores, running handlers and other equipment on the test floor. One of the office girls came out back to smoke a cigarette. I think I was outside finishing up with FedEx at shipping and receiving. So, I stayed, stayed outside to talk with her. As I looked at her, I thought she was pregnant, yet she showed no signs of pregnancy.

So, I asked; are you pregnant as she began to smoke. She said, no why do you ask? I don't think I gave her a clear answer. She later came back a couple or few weeks later saying I am pregnant. A little time after that or that time, she said. I was talking to Elf and asked her what sex my baby would be? Elf, was a Berkeley psychic but told her, a girl or a boy I don't know. She said go ask Mike he's Telepathic he might know. So, this is in the first few weeks or a month of the pregnancy. I was about to say I can't do that, but my thought was interrupted by thinking to say what she wanted. And as I thought that she said a boy, but at that same time I saw a girl. I realized we had had joined as one, at the same moment, thinking the same thought at the same time, yet didn't. I told her I saw a girl; she continued saying she wanted a boy. We sat in the cafeteria with HR in there, I repeated it and why it's a girl, with witnesses there. We had to wait two or three months to find out by ultrasound. Which also said it's a girl and she later had a girl.

Telepathy At a Distance

I was backing my truck up to a client's dock, as I was bumping the dock.

A thought popped into my head that my ex-wife after a few years of separation and divorce was talking with my mother. I did not note the time, because I doubted my mom would remember that specific. But when I got home some hours later, my mom said I talked to your ex wife today. (here name)

Point: I did not know what they talked about, but I know it's possible to know what they talked about. God saw fit, not to give me that ability so I accept that. But I know it's possible to know more. This is the same spirit recorded in the books of God, and no man can prove that it's wrong, by God standards.

Telepathic Projection

Now here's something psychology can really twist the facts on. Further the perpetrator may be listening.3am one morning doing homework, stepped outside to the curb had a cup of coffee. Sprinklers at the school going across the street, sounds muted by it. Thought I heard a sound, but maybe it's just the sprinklers brushing the trees. suddenly I thought I saw something out the side of my eye. I jumped while turning to look and spill my coffee while it splashed. but when I turned to look, I saw nothing and no one.

But Telepathy is like radar, and puts you on remote, so my head turned automatically, and eyes focused on a tree about 50 yards away. I saw a head peering from behind that tree in the distance now it was dark outside, don't forget. A person came creeping out behind a tree and crept to the next tree. Crept from that tree to another in a line of trees, till he was just across from me. Wearing a sack over his head and eyes cut out, carrying a rifle painted white, like ROTC by now as he crept, I crept towards the house and front door from the sidewalk. By the time he was directly across from me he pointed his white rifle at me. I slipped into the house and called the police; I advised them they had a creeping terror on the loose. Two or three minutes later, the area was being swept with spotlights from police cars.

But that's Telepathic projection, like when Archie and I played chess. I saw his arm move in the side of my eye. When I turned to look, I saw the projection of his arm moving. Then I saw his arm move like the image moved. And it was exactly like I saw it.

Telepathy

So, as we study telepathy and being one, in order to think the same thought. So, my girlfriend has started to adjust to my ways, hearing me complain about this or that. So, we ate, and I saw after I had rested see got seconds and another plate. While she was dressing to go to her parents for Christmas, I also got seconds and laid my plate down.

She had come back and sat down. twenty minutes to a half hour pass, I was sitting in one chair her in another. She jumped up and got her plate to take into the kitchen. But, at that same moment I was about to do the same. I simply told her to give it to me, as I also was about to do both plates and she not. See, the thing is, I don't think she saw both plates, so she would not think to take them both, though it's Telepathy.

Telepathy

Many looks upon these things I say as if it's nothing and that's true. But the thing I am showing you can be expanded and become more intense. It's the one thing in our intellect that can be intensified, and you can't see it unless you're looking at it. it requires focus, and you won't understand it.

It can join you to others with such intensity. That in a room of 600 people every time you look at a person, they're looking at you. To such a degree you become paranoid because you start thinking why are they all looking at you? But they're not, you're just joining with everyone that looks at you.

Walk into a room and look straight at the fly on the wall. It's joining you with every living thing.

see1

/sē/

1. perceive with the eyes; discern visually.

espy

2. discern or deduce mentally after reflection or from information; understand.

Extrasensory perception or ESP, also called sixth sense, is a claimed paranormal ability pertaining to reception of information not gained through the recognized physical senses, but sensed with the mind.

"While Peter thought on the vision, the Spirit said unto him, Behold, three men seek thee. Arise therefore, and get thee down, and go with them, doubting nothing: for I have sent them."
Acts 10:19-20 KJV

This is Telepathy being described "See Altogether" with Esdras 6:20

Esdras 6:20,
20 And when the world, that shall begin to vanish away, shall be finished, then will I shew these tokens: the books shall be opened before the firmament, and they shall see all together:
all together (meaning)
phrase of all
all in one place or in a group; all at once

"Unto whom it was revealed, that not unto themselves, but unto us they did minister the things, which are now reported unto you by them that have preached the gospel unto you with the Holy Ghost sent down from heaven, which things the angels desire to look into."
1 Peter 1:12 KJV

So, if UFOs are angels and they come and you have Telepathy, they told you already why they came. And if you see altogether, there probably talking about being put in a trance, having effect worldwide. Just to suppose why you think about a true thing without knowing it's a true thing.

Telesthesia

tel·es·the·sia

the supposed perception of distant occurrences or objects

There came a dream or vision, vision being based in some fact.

I saw the UFO amber set over a street I knew, in a place I knew. I went up into it suddenly and surprised the occupants. A pure black angel, who I seem to be startled when I came to him. He pointed at a machine giving me directions, as if giving me a choice. He began to pray, but his mouth did not move but his voice was heard, he was Telepathic. He said Amen, but I did not acknowledge him, he was angry and tried to shake my hand, I did not, and he yelled Amen I left from before his face passing into a dark place. Were great men held in great darkness called out to me, I went to them. They told me their names kings and presidents long since passed, a man of God confessed to me he was wrong, and they all begged me not to shake that black angel's hand. I left, in those days I was told I was like Adam, by those on the other side. And I looked for those books many years, and things I knew were missing.

Fasting 40 Days is the key to this teaching, particularly of men who might already have Telepathy. Effect of Telepathy are you might also see Satan. See I myself was in about sixty days fast, out of which forty days I may have fasted. Leading to nerve damage other, yes even Telepathy.

1st Book of Adam and Eve 60 (partial)
3 He thus transformed himself in order to deceive Adam and Eve, and to make them come out of the cave, ere they had fulfilled the forty days.
4 For he said within himself, "Now that when they had fulfilled the forty days' fasting and praying,

"And he was there with the LORD forty days and forty nights; he did neither eat bread, nor drink water. And he wrote upon the tables the words of the covenant, the ten commandments. And it came to pass, when Moses came down from mount Sinai with the two tables of testimony.

Telepathy over a distance
Not a good example but illustrates the problems.

Example my girlfriend pulled a post off the internet while at work about a 5-course meal at 09:57am. Not a good example but illustrates the problems.

At, 11:17 I sent a post to a cousin saying my girlfriend always finds these 5 course dinners, maybe my cousin could join us next time. At about 11:20 or so my girlfriend sent me the post she'd downloaded, quite possibly reminded by a Telepathic transmission, from me. Odds are we both thought of it at about 11:17 when I sent the message, but she was busy, so it held her up. I have been in proximity thought a thought at the same time, but because of this or that, I couldn't act immediately watching the other do it.

Critical Thinking
Like the time I was sitting in the living room, and thought I had worms in my weed on a sudden I reached down pulled my weed out from under the couch. I saw nothing! A couple minutes later I saw something glisten in my weed in the box. I looked at it close it was a translucent worm about 1/16 of an inch long. Critical thinking came in after that. I supposed because the cat would lay in my box the worms got into it. Further I had saw little black dried-up worms on the cat before.

Analysis: I never thought any of this until I first knew there were worms in the box, that came after the fact. Further I had telepathic communication with spiders and other insects.

In Moses' hand, when he came down from the mount, that Moses wish not that the skin of his face shone while he talked with him.
Exodus 34:28-29 KJV

"Then was Jesus led up of the Spirit into the wilderness to be tempted of the devil. And when he had fasted forty days and forty nights, he was afterward an hungred."
Matthew 4:1-2 KJV

Telesthesia

tel·es·the·sia

the supposed perception of distant occurrences or objects.

Telepathy

There came a dream or vision, vision being based in some fact. I saw the UFO amber set over a street I knew, in a place I knew. I went up into it suddenly and surprised the occupants. A pure black angel, who I seem to be startled when I came to him. He pointed at a machine giving me directions, as if giving me a choice. He began to pray, but his mouth did not move but his voice was heard, he was Telepathic.

He said Amen, but I did not acknowledge him, he was angry and tried to shake my hand, I did not and he yelled Amen. I left from before his face passing into a dark place. Were great men held in great darkness called out to me, I went to them. They told me their names kings and presidents long since passed, a man of God confessed to me he was wrong, and they all begged me not to shake that black angel's hand. I left, in those days I was told I was like Adam, by those on the other side. And I looked for those books many years, and things I knew were missing.

So, I started doing the research in the Bible and missing books and became pretty good as a researcher. I believe I can show Telepathy, Time Travel who some UFOs are and other things not taught in the mainstream church system, or canon law system. So, I started writing more in my older ages. I started writing songs, stories and screenplays. That was after the school didn't post my records with the state, and held my degree, putting a forgery on me, after they lost their accreditation and closed.

But by now I was well into the study of Telepathy. But it seemed I knew things in the Bible were missing. Particularly it did make any since to have a war in heaven and them not use ships. So my study was looking for that first and foremost, thinking if I find that, I'll find the ships. But to me it was as if something was leading me to the missing books. I seemed to know what I would find before I found it.

"Having then gifts differing according to the grace that is given to us, whether prophecy, let us prophesy according to the proportion of faith;"
Romans 12:6 KJV (in part)

"For who maketh thee to differ from another? and what hast thou that thou didst not receive? now if thou didst receive it, why dost thou glory, as if thou hadst not received it?"
1 Corinthians 4:7 KJV (in part)

Point is this, these things might affect every person differently and that may be a problem for science. Science assumes that objects and events in natural systems occur in consistent patterns that are understandable through measurement and observation.

Here Nebuchadnezzar joined with beast and became one, until his hair was matted. It's a case of Telepathy but few know it. It thought which can join you with anything, or most living things.

"let his heart be changed from man's, and let a beast's heart be given unto him; and let seven times pass over him. This matter is by the decree of the watchers, and the demand by the word of the holy ones: to the intent that the living may know that the most High ruleth in the kingdom of men, and giveth it to whomsoever he will, and setteth up over it the basest of men."
Daniel 4:16-17 KJV (in part)

The same hour was the thing fulfilled upon Nebuchadnezzar: and he was driven from men, and did eat grass as oxen, and his body was wet with the dew of heaven, till his hairs were grown like eagles' feathers, and his nails like birds' claws.
Daniel 4:16, 33 KJV

So, he suffered from something which joined him with beast. So as we study telepathy and being one, in order to think the same thought. So, my girlfriend has started to adjust to my ways, hearing me complain about this or that. So, we ate, and I saw after I had rested see got seconds and another plate. While she was dressing to go to her parents for Christmas, I also got seconds and laid my plate down. She had come back and sat down.

Twenty minutes to a half hour pass, I was sitting in one chair her in another. she jumped up and got her plate to take into the kitchen. But, at that same moment I was about to do the same. I simply told her to give it to me, as I also was about to do both plates and she not. See, the thing is, I don't think she saw both plates, so she would not think to take them both, though it's Telepathy

Telepathy

Here's the thing, when I speak of the Spirit or Telepathy joining you with every living thing, I mean it. Me and the Spider. I laid down to sleep for the night. But I kept feeling the uneasiness and could not sleep. This feeling kept occurring for a few times as I looked over my shoulder again and again.

(A) I also saw a dark arm in a red lit place taring off a piece of raw meat to some degree. I finally rolled over on my back and saw a big spider hanging from the ceiling about 8 inches over my head.

(B) Do spiders eat meat?

Science Says

All the spiders in the world eat more meat per year than humans do. Spiders scoff between 400 and 800 million metric tones of insect meat and other "prey kill." That's up to twice as much as people eat.

(C) Do spiders see in color?

At the time I had a red light on in my room, so if you ask me, I'm sure spiders see red.

Science Says

Many spiders may also have a crude form of color vision, but for them it's usually based on green and ultraviolet light, which extends their vision into the deep violet end of the spectrum beyond what humans can see and covers the blue and purple hues in between. But some jumping spiders see even more.

These spiders jumped, another like it was in the corner above the bath tub, as I was washing the tube out, I knew it would jump on me. Moving my arm quickly away. The spider jumped into the hot water and went down the drain.

EPIGRAPH

Well, if I'm to make sense of this dream. Sorry as I was working, I realized part of this story wasn't told. Back to work I got distracted. Here's the thing, the Archimedes Spiral might make sense. According to the teaching the whole order of Grigori fell. If I saw a Grigori he was fallen, yet he was Telepathic and gave me something. Black like a polished pitch-black smooth stone.

Telepathic his mouth didn't move yet he talked. I saw a UFO and went up into it. He jumped shocked when I came, and he immediately Prayed. He said Amen; I just looked at him and he yelled Amen again at me. He reached to shake my hand, and I rejected it. He grew angry,

He then pointed at a machine or computer and showed me the Archimedes Spiral, which I had no knowledge of this symbol till forty and something years later. But at the same Time as I was leaving, voices of men called me. I heard them held in darkness, went to them a great many of great men of the earth called to me. I talked to some, saying their names. Seems they knew me somehow. Great men, Presidents, and Kings and like those of great fame, held by that Grigori.

Further, I knew Satan was black, 20, 30 or 40 years before reading it. How did I know about the Archimedes Spiral something I never saw nor was taught? For years I looked for it since the end of 1970's that's how I know I never saw it. And was young enough to remember I was never taught it. How did I know Satan had a UFO before I began to study it?

I just found its meaning 03/08/2023. Telepathy is, Archimedes Spiral is a factual thing I saw it, without ever being taught it, or seeing it before. How did I know Satan was Black without being taught? Well, maybe that Grigori implied he had Archimedes held in that place as well?

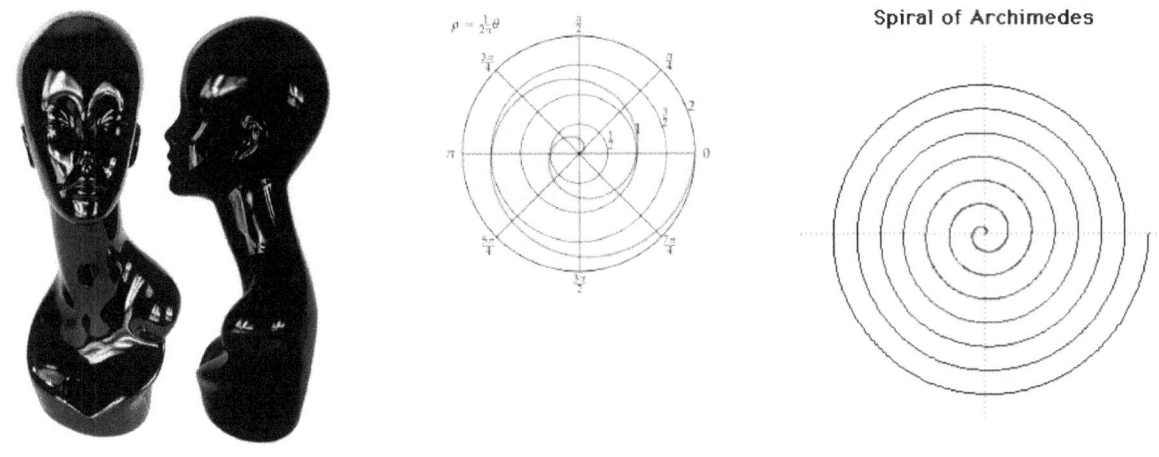

It's my belief I was walking in the spirit of the Lord I was seeing something Christ saw when he descended into the depths so to speak. It reminds me of the book of Isaiah.

"Hell from beneath is moved for thee to meet thee at thy coming: it stirreth up the dead for thee, even all the chief ones of the earth; it hath raised up from their thrones all the kings of the nations." Isaiah 14:9 KJV

It's almost as if I was walking in this place.

CHAPTER 9
THRONE

THE ARCHIMEDES PALIMPSEST PROJECT, perhaps this writing being deciphered has the clues to why a fallen Angel would point at this?

ABOUT THE ARCHIMEDES PALIMPSEST
The Archimedes Palimpsest is a medieval parchment manuscript, now consisting of 174 parchment folios. While it contains no less than seven treatises by Archimedes, calling it the Archimedes Palimpsest is a little confusing. As it is now, the manuscript is a Byzantine prayerbook, written in Greek, and technically called a euchologion. This euchologion was completed by April 1229, and was probably made in Jerusalem.

The prayer book, or Euchologion, is itself of some interest, and further information on its contents can be discovered in this website. However, to make their prayer book, the scribes used parchment that had already been used for the writings of other books. The books they took parchment from were as follows.

Throne to me, can be associated with Time Travel sure enough. But certainly, a vessel of some type. Most likely there are some capable of causing reactions such as "Higgs Boson's God Particle Reactions". But these particles are all the elements in existence and how they first existed in the physical. I believe Gods throne is capable of such. Because if you jump back in time before all things existed, even a spirit or soul. You require the capability to create spirits and souls. A spirit by definition here, is the thing that forms the physical thing, which when it forms represents a thing. Thrones manipulate the physical. Cause weather events. Thrones manipulate time.

"For thou hast said in thine heart, I will ascend into heaven, I will exalt my throne above the stars of God: I will sit also upon the mount of the congregation, in the sides of the north:"
Isaiah 14:13 KJV

What is Heaven?

If you notice great means big in many cases, such as great lights which appear as ships. Yet people are taught to perceive such, different than they are written.

First there are problems with this text, if you believe Adam to be the first man, and the dead won't be raised until the second coming.

Why do we see young men before the resurrection? See so Deductive Reasoning will tell you the only way that can be accomplished is through Time Travel. And though they are telling us they broke the Time Barrier people still reject what's written.

Notice the great light could mean big light or UFO which came to the tomb, yet this teaching has been overthrown by lesser beliefs which actually make men blind to the truth.

The Lost Gospel According to Peter
9 And in the night in which the Lord's Day was drawing on, as the soldiers kept guard two by two in a watch, there was a great voice in the heaven; and they saw the heavens opened, and two men descend from thence with great light and approach the tomb. And that stone which was put at the door rolled of itself and made way in part; and the tomb was opened, and both the young men entered in.

"And let them be for lights in the firmament of the heaven to give light upon the earth: and it was so. And God made two great lights; the greater light to rule the day, and the lesser light to rule the night: he made the stars also."
Genesis 1:15-16 KJV

Satan's Star
2 And behold a single star fell from heaven.

3 Which being raised up, ate and fed among those cows.

4 After that I perceived other large and black cows; and behold all of them changed their stalls and pastures, while their young began to lament one with another. Again I looked in my vision, and surveyed heaven; when behold I saw many stars which descended, and projected themselves from heaven to where the first star was,

Great light means large light, large in size and magnitude.

great
/grāt/
 Learn to pronounce
adjective
1.of an extent, amount, or intensity considerably above the normal or average.
2.of ability, quality, or eminence considerably above the normal or average.

Now look at Satan light; "Great Light" big light could be its meaning. Just because men say its not the meaning, you must consider those men's motives and belief and power. What do they have to lose by the truth being known?

It's Book of Adam and Eve

2 He began with transforming his hosts; in his hands was a flashing fire, and they were in a great light.

3 He then placed his throne near the mouth of the cave because he could not enter into it by reason of their prayers. And he shed light into the cave, until the cave glistened over Adam and Eve, while his hosts began to sing praises.

4 And Satan did this, in order that when Adam saw the light, he should think within himself that it was a heavenly light, and that Satan's hosts were angels; and that God had sent them to watch at the cave, and to give him light in the darkness.

What is the shape of a throne.

Enoch 14

17 Attentively I surveyed it, and saw that it contained an exalted throne.

18 The appearance of which was like that of frost; while its circumference resembled the orb of the brilliant sun; and there was the voice of the cherubim.

cir·cum·fer·ence
/sərˈkəmf(ə)rəns/
Learn to pronounce
noun
the enclosing boundary of a curved geometric figure, especially a circle.

Satan Black

Secrets of Enoch 7

AND those men took me and led me up on to the second heaven, and showed me darkness, greater than earthly darkness, and there I saw prisoners hanging, watched, awaiting the great and boundless judgement, and these angels were dark-looking, more than earthly darkness, and incessantly making weeping through all hours.

2nd Book of Adam and Eve 4

3 And God said to Adam, "Look at this devil, and at his hideous look, and know that he it is who made thee fall from brightness into darkness, from peace and rest to toil and misery.

4 And look, O Adam, at him, who said of himself that he is God! Can God be black? Would God take the form of a woman? Is there any one stronger than God? And can He be overpowered?

Secrets of Enoch 7

AND those men took me and led me up on to the second heaven, and showed me darkness, greater than earthly darkness, and there I saw prisoners hanging, watched, awaiting the great and

boundless judgement, and these angels were dark-looking, more than earthly darkness, and incessantly making weeping through all hours.

2nd Book of Adam and Eve 4
3 And God said to Adam, "Look at this devil, and at his hideous look, and know that he it is who made thee fall from brightness into darkness, from peace and rest to toil and misery.
4 And look, O Adam, at him, who said of himself that he is God! Can God be black? Would God take the form of a woman? Is there any one stronger than God? And can He be overpowered?
Thing is I fasted like Adam and got Telepathy 40 days, I knew Satan was black and all these things twenty years before reading it.

Not by your interpretation, but by the books of God.

"And I looked, and behold, a whirlwind came out of the north, a great cloud, and a fire infoldings itself, and a brightness was about it, and out of the midst thereof as the color of amber, out of the midst of the fire."
Ezekiel 1:4 KJV

"Then I beheld, and lo a likeness as the appearance of fire: from the appearance of his loins even downward, fire; and from his loins even upward, as the appearance of brightness, as the color of amber."
Ezekiel 8:2 KJV

"And above the firmament that was over their heads was the likeness of a throne, as the appearance of a sapphire stone: and upon the likeness of the throne was the likeness as the appearance of a man above upon it. And I saw as the color of amber, as the appearance of fire round about within it, from the appearance of his loins even upward, and from the appearance of his loins even downward, I saw as it were the appearance of fire, and it had brightness round about. As the appearance of the bow that is in the cloud in the day of rain, so was the appearance of the brightness round about. This was the appearance of the likeness of the glory of the LORD. And when I saw it, I fell upon my face, and I heard a voice of one that spake."

Ezekiel 1:26-28 KJV

round about

phrase of round

1. on all sides or in all directions; surrounding someone or something.

"everything round about was covered with snow"

2. at a point or time approximately equal to.

EVIDENCE TIME STOPPED ZERO TIME SHOWN

Protevangelion 13

AND leaving her and his sons in the cave, Joseph went forth to seek a Hebrew midwife in the village of Bethlehem.

2 But as I was going (said Joseph) I looked up into the air, and I saw the clouds astonished, and the fowls of the air stopping in the midst of their flight.

3 And I looked down towards the earth, and saw a table spread, and working people sitting around it, but their hands were upon the table, and they did not move to eat.

4 They who had meat in their mouths did not eat.

5 They who lifted their hands up to their heads did not draw them back:

6 And they who lifted them up to their mouths did not put anything in;

7 But all their faces were fixed upwards.

8 And I beheld the sheep dispersed, and yet the sheep stood still.

9 And the shepherd lifted up his hand to smite them, and his hand continued up.

10 And I looked unto a river and saw the kids with their mouths close to the water, and touching it, but they did not drink.

Protevangelion 14

9 And the midwife went along with him, and stood in the cave.

10 Then a bright cloud overshadowed the cave, and the midwife said, This day my soul is magnified, for mine eyes have seen surprising things, and salvation is brought forth to Israel.

11 But on a sudden the cloud became a great light in the cave, so that their eyes could not bear it.

12 But the light gradually decreased, until the infant appeared, and sucked the breast of his mother Mary.

FORM OF THE STAR

Protevangelion 15

7 They answered him, We saw an extraordinary large star shining among the stars of heaven, and so out-shined all the other stars, as that they became not visible, and we knew thereby that a great king was born in Israel, and therefore we are come to worship him.

Form of the Star

2 Then the Lady Mary took one of his swaddling clothes in which the infant was wrapped, and gave it to them instead of a blessing, which they received from her as a most noble present.

3 And at the same time there appeared to them an angel in the form of that star which had before been their guide in their journey; the light of which they followed till they returned into their own country.

Birth of Abraham

Jasher 8

2 And when all the wise men and conjurors went out from the house of Terah, they lifted up their eyes toward heaven that night to look at the stars, and they saw, and behold one very large star came from the east and ran in the heavens, and he swallowed up the four stars from the four sides of the heavens.

3 And all the wise men of the king and his conjurors were astonished at the sight, and the sages understood this matter, and they knew its import.

From The War In Heaven

As to what I think, correct or incorrect we will see. It appears after the creation of man, there rose up a power against man, because God would come from man.

So, it would seem Christ becoming God, and taken early. To me would alter Time to such a degree, it would cause a continuous Time loop. If repeated again and again.

So, if Christ is who created heaven and earth, in order to stop the Time loop and cause an end to that loop. Another person would have to be resurrected in his place at the end.

So, it's my belief Michael is put in place, to break the Time Loop (instead of Christ being raised perhaps Michael is put in place to stop the Time Loop or creation repeating again and again. This is probably what Satan caused jumping back in Time to destroy man. To stop Christ from coming into existence and becoming God.

So, if Christ is the son of David, then it would not be possible to put another in Mary. You see that would cause a Time Loop having no end. Then the process would continue Time and Time again. Causing a Time Loop without an end.

The Pillar of a Cloud and Cloud
1st Book of Adam and Eve 28
But when the wily Satan saw them, that they were going to the garden, he gathered together his host, and came in appearance upon a cloud, intent on deceiving them.
1st Book of Adam and Eve 60
23 "God said further to me, 'If thou hast not strength to walk, I will send a cloud to carry thee and alight thee at the entrance of their cave; then the cloud will return and leave thee there.
24 "'And if they will come with thee, I will send a cloud to carry thee and them.'
25 "Then He commanded a cloud, and it bare me up and brought me to you; and then went back.

"And the LORD appeared in the tabernacle in a pillar of a cloud: and the pillar of the cloud stood over the door of the tabernacle."
Deuteronomy 31:15 KJV

"And Moses went into the midst of the cloud, and gat him up into the mount: and Moses was in the mount forty days and forty nights."
Exodus 24:18 KJV

gat2
/gat/
verb
verb: gat
archaic past of get.

Protevangelion 14
10 Then a bright cloud overshadowed the cave, and the midwife
said, this day my soul is magnified, for mine eyes have seen surprising things, and salvation is brought forth to Israel.
11 But on a sudden the cloud became a great light in the cave, so that their eyes could not bear it.
12 But the light gradually decreased, until the infant appeared, and sucked the breast of his mother Mary.

The Pillar of a Cloud and Cloud
1st Book of Adam and Eve 28
BUT when the wily Satan saw them, that they were going to the garden, he gathered together his host, and came in appearance upon a cloud, intent on deceiving them.

1st Book of Adam and Eve 60
23 "God said further to me, 'If thou hast not strength to walk, I will send a cloud to carry thee and alight thee at the entrance of their cave; then the cloud will return and leave thee there.
24 "'And if they will come with thee, I will send a cloud to carry thee and them.'
25 "Then He commanded a cloud, and it bare me up and brought me to you; and then went back.

Protevangelion 13

AND leaving her and his sons in the cave, Joseph went forth to seek a Hebrew midwife in the village of Bethlehem.

2 But as I was going (said Joseph) I looked up into the air, and I saw the clouds astonished, and the fowls of the air stopping in the midst of their flight.

3 And I looked down towards the earth, and saw a table spread, and working people sitting around it, but their hands were upon the table, and they did not move to eat.

4 They who had meat in their mouths did not eat.

"But Peter and they that were with him were heavy with sleep: and when they were awake, they saw his glory, and the two men that stood with him. And it came to pass, as they departed from him, Peter said unto Jesus, Master, it is good for us to be here: and let us make three tabernacles; one for thee, and one for Moses, and one for Elias: not knowing what he said. While he thus spake, there came a cloud, and overshadowed them: and they feared as they entered into the cloud. And there came a voice out of the cloud, saying, this is my beloved Son: hear him. And when the voice was past, Jesus was found alone. And they kept it close and told no man in those days any of those things which they had seen."

Luke 9:32-36 KJV

"and was transfigured before them: and his face did shine as the sun, and his raiment was white as the light. And, behold, there appeared unto them Moses and Elias talking with him. Then answered Peter, and said unto Jesus, Lord, it is good for us to be here: if thou wilt, let us make here three tabernacles; one for thee, and one for Moses, and one for Elias. While he yet spake, behold, a bright cloud overshadowed them: and behold a voice out of the cloud, which said, This is my beloved Son, in whom I am well pleased; hear ye him. And when the disciples heard it, they fell on their face, and were sore afraid. And Jesus came and touched them, and said, Arise, and be not afraid. And when they had lifted up their eyes, they saw no man, save Jesus only. And as they came down from the mountain, Jesus charged them, saying, Tell the vision to no man, until the Son of man be risen again from the dead."

Matthew 17:2-9 KJV

"And his raiment became shining, exceeding white as snow; so as no fuller on earth can white them. And there appeared unto them Elias with Moses: and they were talking with Jesus. And Peter answered and said to Jesus, Master, it is good for us to be here: and let us make three tabernacles; one for thee, and one for Moses, and one for Elias. For he wist not what to say; for they were sore afraid. And there was a cloud that overshadowed them: and a voice came out of the cloud, saying, This is my beloved Son: hear him. And suddenly, when they had looked round about, they saw no man anymore, save Jesus only with themselves. And as they came down from the mountain, he charged them that they should tell no man what things they had seen, till the Son of man were risen from the dead."

Mark 9:3-9 KJV

"And the LORD appeared in the tabernacle in a pillar of a cloud: and the pillar of the cloud stood over the door of the tabernacle."

Deuteronomy 31:15 KJV

"And Moses went into the midst of the cloud, and gat him up into the mount: and Moses was in the mount forty days and forty nights."

Exodus 24:18 KJV

gat2

/gat/

verb

verb: gat

archaic past of get.

EPIGRAPH

What is the dimensions of Time?

Times: extent is what is past, what is now, what is to come.

-which extents could be forever

Zero Time:

If there is motion there without time?

If motion without time is possible how much more can be accomplished in a single point in time.

Fact is: I believe UFO's could interact with us and we not see them simply existing in the same space but at different times, like how we live in a place day to day, yet at different times.

No time calculation, not occupying space and time.

Example: if you get up and move out of a chair.

I as a time traveler, I come sit in your chair two minutes after you get up.

1- I would have to enter your room a zero time so as to not affect the time you are in.

(A) If I could alter all time, and I jump back in Time all time would adjust and go back to the day I went to. But to disrupt this effect you enter with zero time. Co existing with Time, without disrupting time must be a possibility if time travel exist.

Solution = to zero time can inter time and not alter actual time or linear time.

di·men·sion

/dəˈmen(t)SH(ə)n/

noun

plural noun: dimensions

1.a measurable extent of some kind, such as length, breadth, depth, or height.

CHAPTER 10
SOME RESURRECTED WERE PERHAPS NOT YET BORN

Here's the thing because time is stuck together, people show up at the resurrection that may not have been born. I found some of the Archangels but, not all of them, I think Michael of the Old Testament, may be Michael the archangel, I don't know. Fact is some of the stuff shown me Telepathically, makes it hard to conclude. Certainly, he is an angel, but the question is arch Angel since many things written are for the end of days.
(Revelation 20: 4 - 6 broken up)

"And when he had opened the fifth seal, I saw under the altar the souls of them that were slain for the word of God, and for the testimony which they held: and they cried with a loud voice, saying, how long, O Lord, holy and true, dost thou not judge and avenge our blood on them that dwell on the earth? And white robes were given unto every one of them; and it was said unto them, that they should rest yet for a little season, until their fellow servants also and their brethren, that should be killed as they were, should be fulfilled. Please, note these are those of the first taken and will be with him in the eight day prior to the whole earth being resurrected. Many of these are those who appear in the books removed.
The Secrets of Enoch 35

TIME STUCK TOGETHER

Letters of Herod and Pilot
Now when he was crucified, there was darkness over all the world, and the sun was obscured for half a day, and the stars appeared, but no lustre was seen in them; and the moon lost its brightness, as though tinged with blood; and the world of the departed was swallowed up; so that the very

sanctuary of the temple, as they call it, did not appear to the Jews themselves at their fall, but they perceived a chasm in the earth, and the rolling of successive thunders.

And amid this terror the dead appeared rising again, as the Jews themselves bore witness, and said that it was Abraham, and Isaac, and Jacob, and the twelve patriarchs, and Moses, and Job, who had died before, as they say, some three thousand five hundred years.
And there were very many whom I myself saw appearing in the body, and they made lamentation over the Jews, because of the transgression, which was committed by them, and because of the destruction of the Jews and of their law. So again, because Time is Stuck Together, and all things become seven time's stronger themselves. The angel are required to contain some things to preserve life on earth. As I have stated fires might burn out of control if Oxygen isn't contained or held back.

And the terror of the earthquake continued from the sixth hour of the preparation until the ninth hour; and when it was evening on the first day of the week, there came a sound from heaven, and the heaven became seven times more luminous than on all other days. And at the third hour of the night the sun appeared more luminous than it had ever shone, lighting up the whole hemisphere.

And as lightning-flashes suddenly come forth in a storm, so there were seen men, lofty in stature, and surpassing in glory, a countless host, crying out, and their voice was heard as that of exceedingly loud thunder, Jesus that was crucified is risen again: come up from Hades ye that were enslaved in the subterraneous recesses of Hades.

And the chasm in the earth was as if it had no bottom; but it was so that the very foundations of the earth appeared, with those that shouted in heaven, and walked in the body among the dead that were raised. And He that raised up all the dead and bound Hades said, say to my disciples He goeth before you into Galilee, there shall ye see Him. And all that night the light ceased not shining.

And many of the Jews died in the chasm of the earth, being swallowed up, so that on the morrow most of those who had been against Jesus were not to be found. Others saw the apparition of men rising again whom none of us had ever seen. One synagogue of the Jews was alone left in Jerusalem itself, for they all disappeared in that ruin.

Now when he was crucified darkness came over all the world; the sun was altogether hidden, and the sky appeared dark while it was yet day, so that the stars were seen, though still they had their lustre obscured, wherefore, I suppose your excellency is not unaware that in all the world they lighted their lamps from the sixth hour until evening. And the moon, which was like blood, did not shine all night long, although it was at the full, and the stars and Orion made lamentation over the

BEHOLD from their seed shall arise another generation, much afterwards, but of them many will be very insatiate.
2 He who raises that generation, shall reveal to them the books of thy handwriting, of thy fathers, to them to whom he must point out the guardianship of the world, to the faithful men and workers of my pleasure, who do not acknowledge my name in vain.
3 And they shall tell another generation, and those others having read shall be glorified thereafter, more than the first.

Someone is supposed to point out the guardianship of the world. I believe this is Christ or the Son who does this. And this is how Michael would rise to power. This is of course if Christ is he who sits on the throne. Well God, I understand things two ways. If Christ created all things, he did not create the father. Why? Because the Father is self-eternal. What does that mean? God the father does not require creation, he can create himself. Just questions.

But, if Christ did create the Father, it would be, because of a "Time Jump" or that he moved so fast he became two by looping Time? But it's easier to believe he's self-eternal and requires no assistance. I would say Adam is the father had not been for this verse that says.
"Not that any man hath seen the Father, save he which is of God, he hath seen the Father."
John 6:46 KJV
The thing is perhaps no one has seen what Adam was changed to look like after the resurrection.
Adam was probably in heaven because of time travel, be the time Christ was sent, having come from beyond the eight day, so no telling, it's a question?

Though I believe if Christ is in-fact the Ancient of Days, (a possibility at least). This is done to break the Time Loop of Christ having to repeat coming to earth again and again. Because Satan and his angels jumped back in Time. Another must replace him, but because he isn't the son of David, cannot be sent back in Time, breaking a Time loop.
(Revelation continued)

"And I saw thrones, and they sat upon them, and judgment was given unto them: and I saw the souls of them that were beheaded for the witness of Jesus, and for the word of God, and which had not worshipped the beast, neither his image, neither had received his mark upon their foreheads, or in their hands; and they lived and reigned with Christ a thousand years.
So, what this is saying in the eighth day Christ was raised from the dead. Christ being the first fruit was sent back to be Christ. (Who he was before sent back to be Christ we know is the Question. Fact is he is said to be the son of David)

But he is also He which created all things. So, Christ being raised had to have created all things after that? But during this Time after the first resurrection Christ and his angels reign in earths future.

But if he created all things, all things would start again. This will create a Time Loop if Christ comes again as a man. This is of course if he now became the Ancient of Days. Which might also mean no man had ever seen him, because all those created after this were now gone. Because he went back in Time all things created vanished, and he remade all things. So, no man would in that case know him. Particularly if man is a new creation after that.

But the rest of the dead lived not again until the thousand years were finished. This is the first resurrection. Blessed and holy is he that hath part in the first resurrection: on such the second death hath no power, but they shall be priests of God and of Christ and shall reign with him a thousand years."
Revelation 20:4-6 KJV

So, these are some of those who reign with Christ in the first resurrection. These are those raised in the eighth day, but yet appeared at the Resurrection of Christ with him. Even some of them, may not have been born yet.

These are those sent back in Time and gave us all the Holy Books of God through Time travel, even the Bible.

The Gospel according to Peter
9 And in the night in which the Lord's Day was drawing on, as the soldiers kept guard two by two in a watch, there was a great voice in the heaven; and they saw the heavens opened, and two men descend from thence with great light and approach the tomb.
And that stone which was put at the door rolled of itself and made way in part; and the tomb was opened, and both the young men entered in.
10 When therefore those soldiers saw it, they awakened the centurion and the elders; for they too were hard by keeping guard.
And as they declared what things they had seen, again they see three men come forth from the tomb,

Enoch 17
1 They raised me up into a certain place, where there was the appearance of a burning fire; and when they pleased, they assumed the likeness of men

"Blessed and holy is he that hath part in the first resurrection: on such the second death hath no power, but they shall be priests of God and of Christ and shall reign with him a thousand years."
Revelation 20:6 KJV

"And of the angels he saith, Who maketh his angels spirits, And his ministers a flame of fire."
Hebrews 1:7 KJV

"Who maketh his angels' spirits; His ministers a flaming fire:"
Psalm 104:4 KJV

Raphael is an example of a resurrected angel being sent back in Time after the resurrection as his minister. Like also is Judges 13:19, 20 his ministers a flaming fire.

"So Manoah took a kid with a meat offering, and offered it upon a rock unto the LORD: and the angel did wondrously; and Manoah and his wife looked on. For it came to pass, when the flame went up toward heaven from off the altar, that the angel of the LORD ascended in the flame of the altar. And Manoah and his wife looked on it, and fell on their faces to the ground."
Judges 13:19-20 KJV

Tobit 12
15 I am Raphael, one of the seven holy angels, which present the prayers of the saints, and which go in and out before the glory of the Holy One.

THIS IS THE EIGHTH DAY
Revelation continued
And I beheld when he had opened the sixth seal, and, lo, there was a great earthquake; and the sun became black as sackcloth of hair, and the moon became as blood; and the stars of heaven fell unto the earth, even as a fig tree casteth her untimely figs, when she is shaken of a mighty wind.

And the heaven departed as a scroll when it is rolled together; and every mountain and island were moved out of their places.
Revelation 6:9-14 KJV

So, suppose during this thousand-year period, those of us resurrected during the first resurrection are required to save what flesh we can. This is the prophecy of such things.

"And after these things I saw four angels standing on the four corners of the earth, holding the four winds of the earth, that the wind should not blow on the earth, nor on the sea, nor on any tree. And I saw another angel ascending from the east, having the seal of the living God: and he cried with

a loud voice to the four angels, to whom it was given to hurt the earth and the sea, saying, hurt not the earth, neither the sea, nor the trees, till we have sealed the servants of our God in their foreheads. And I heard the number of them which were sealed: and there were sealed a hundred and forty and four thousand of all the tribes of the children of Israel."
Revelation 7:1-4 KJV

Jews, because of the transgression committed by them. And on the first day of the week, about the third hour of the night, the sun appeared as it never shone before, and the whole heaven became bright. And as lightnings come in a storm, so certain men of lofty stature, in beautiful array, and of indescribable glory, appeared in the air, and a countless host of angels, crying out and saying, Glory to God in the highest, and on earth peace, good will among men: Come up from Hades, ye who are in bondage in the depths of Hades.

And at their voice all the mountains and hills were moved, and the rocks were rent, and great chasms were made in the earth, so that the very places of the abyss were visible.

And amid the terror dead men were seen rising again, so that the Jews who saw it said, We beheld Abraham and Isaac, and Jacob, and the twelve patriarchs, who died some two thousand five hundred years before, and we beheld Noah clearly in the body. And all the multitude walked about and sang hymns to God with a loud voice, saying, The Lord our God, who hath risen from the dead, hath made alive all the dead, and Hades he hath spoiled and slain.

Therefore, my lord king, all that night the light ceased not. But many of the Jews died, and were sunk and swallowed up in the chasms that night, so that not even their bodies were to be seen. Now I mean, that those of the Jews suffered who spake against Jesus. And but one synagogue remained in Jerusalem, for all the synagogues which had been against Jesus were overwhelmed.

Through that terror, therefore, being amazed and being seized with great trembling, in that very hour, I ordered what had been done by them all to be written, and I have sent it to thy mightiness. So, this is what will happen when Time is Stuck together to make no Time. The dead will be raised, and we will be resurrected.

Well, I need no judgment of men, God will judge me. If I am wrong, he will punish me as a false prophet. But I study his work, and by his teaching I teach. I seek redemption to God, if required I fall on my sword. Or I pick up his cross and bear it. But I tell you, before you say I'm wrong look again at the books which say you are wrong, in God's name Amen.

Also note that angel ascending from the east is a man being resurrected and one of those given a throne and guardianship of the earth Archangel most likely.

/set/

1. put, lay, or stand (something) in a specified place or position.

"Dana set the mug of tea down."

Similar:

2. put or bring into a specified state.

EPIGRAPH

Time Stuck together.

Time Stuck Together; water being pulled from the future to cause the flood. Each of the seven cataract is in a thousand-year period of the earth water. Or basically 7 times as much or 7-thousand-year periods is where the water on the earth is coming from. If you pull water for 7000 millennium from under the earth at the same time. 7 times more water would rise, to flood the earth using water from a different period.

Jasher 6

11 And on that day, the Lord caused the whole earth to shake, and the sun darkened, and the foundations of the world raged, and the whole earth was moved violently, and the lightning flashed, and the thunder roared, and all the fountains in the earth were broken up, such as was not known to the inhabitants before; and God did this mighty act, in order to terrify the sons of men, that there might be no more evil upon earth.

12 And still the sons of men would not return from their evil ways, and they increased the anger of the Lord at that time and did not even direct their hearts to all this.

13 And at the end of seven days, in the six hundredth year of the life of Noah, the waters of the flood were upon the earth.

14 And all the fountains of the deep were broken up, and the windows of heaven were opened, and the rain was upon the earth forty days and forty nights.

Enoch 88

2 Again I lifted my eyes towards heaven and saw a lofty roof. Above it were seven cataracts, which poured forth on a certain village much water.

9 Again I looked in the vision until those cataracts from that lofty roof were removed, and the fountains of the earth became equalized, while other depths were opened.

10 Into which the water began to descend, until the dry ground appeared.

CHAPTER 11
CREATION / SCIENCE

How long was it light?

We always see the Big Bang's leftover glow in all directions in space; it never goes away. On the other hand, light from the Big Bang is still visible today, even though the Big Bang itself occurred 13.8 billion years ago. This allowed light to finally shine through, about 380,000 years after the Big Bang. How long is the light with God? And God calls it a great age where light is born from light.

THE FIRST DAY

GOD

Secrets of Enoch 25

I COMMANDED in the very lowest parts, that visible things should come down from invisible, and Adoil came down very great, and I beheld him, and lo! he had a belly of great light.

2 And I said to him: 'Become undone, Adoil, and let the visible come out of thee.'

3 And he came undone, and a great light came out. And I was in the midst of the great light, and as there is born light from light, there came forth a great age, and showed all creation, which I had thought to create.

"And God said, Let there be light: and there was light. And God saw the light, that it was good: and God divided the light from the darkness."
Genesis 1:3-4 KJV

SCIENCE

How long was there darkness after the Big Bang?

How long was it dark?

We now know when cosmic dawn ended. For a period of roughly 100 million years in the early universe, starting about 380,000 years after the big bang, the cosmos was completely dark.

In Big Bang cosmology, shortly after the blazingly bright Big Bang itself, there came a time when the universe was utterly dark. This period, before the first stars were born, and is thought to have lasted several hundred million years in our 13.8-billion-year-old universe. Astronomers call it the Cosmic Dark Ages.

How did matter form after the Big Bang?
Many of the bosons around just after the big bang were so energetic that they could decay into much more massive particles such as protons (remember, $E=mc^2$, so to make a particle with a large mass m, you need a boson with a high energy E). The mass in the universe came from such decays.

THE SECOND DAY

GOD

Secrets of Enoch 27

AND I commanded that there should be taken from light and darkness, and I said: 'Be thick,' and it became thus and I spread it out with the light, and it became water, and I spread it out over the darkness, below the light, and then I made firm the waters, that is to say the bottomless, and I made foundation of light around the water, and created seven circles from inside, and imaged it (sc. the water) like crystal wet and dry, that is to say like glass, and the circumcession of the waters and the other elements, and I showed each one of them its road, and the seven stars each one of them in its heaven, that they go thus, and I saw that it was good.

2 And I separated between light and between darkness, that is to say in the midst of the water hither and thither, and I said to the light, that it should be the day, and to the darkness, that it should be the night, and there was evening and there was morning the first day.

SCIENCE

That's what's being described here.

The Higgs boson is the fundamental particle associated with the Higgs field, a field that gives mass to other fundamental particles such as electrons and quarks. A particle's mass determines how much it resists changing its speed or position when it encounters a force. Not all fundamental particles have mass.

Where did mass come from big bang?
During the very first moments of the universe, almost all particles were massless, traveling at the speed of light in a very hot "primordial soup." At some point during this period, the Higgs field turned on, permeating the universe and giving mass to the elementary particles.

The universe bathes in a sea of light, from the blue-white flickering of young stars to the deep red glow of hydrogen clouds.

So, let's compare this Timeline with Gods Creation. It appears hydrogen clouds would be red, so up to know Enoch and scientists appear to be on the same page. And they both call them ages.

So, once again it appears those who won't accept these books, though claiming to be men of God. Are in fact, doing damage to the teaching of God, by rejecting the books of God.

GOD
Jubilees 2
Angels of the presence, and the angels of sanctification, and the angels of the spirit of the winds, and the angels of the spirit of the clouds, and of darkness, and of snow and of hail and of hoar frost, and the angels of the voices and of the thunder and of the lightning, and the angels of the spirits of cold and of heat, and of winter and of spring and of autumn and of summer, and of all the spirits of His creatures which are in the heavens and on the earth, the abysses and the darkness, eventide and the light, dawn and day, which He hath prepared in the knowledge of His heart. 3. And thereupon we saw His works, and praised Him, and lauded before Him on account of all His works; for seven great works did He create on the first day. 4. And on the second day

SCIENCE

The Sun and the planets formed together, 4.6 billion years ago, from a cloud of gas and dust called the solar nebula. A shock wave from a nearby supernova explosion probably initiated the collapse of the solar nebula. The Sun formed in the center, and the planets formed in a thin disk orbiting around it.

There have been many estimates for when the earth's inner core was formed, but scientists from the University of Liverpool have used new data which indicates that the Earth's inner core was formed 1 -- 1.5 billion years ago as it "froze" from the surrounding molten iron outer core.

This increased magnetic field is a likely indication of the first occurrence of solid iron at Earth's Centre and the point in Earth's history at which the solid inner core first started to "freeze" out from the cooling molten outer core.

So, the Bottomless is the core by this definition in Secrets of Enoch 27 and 28 also called the first day. And extensive period from big bang and darkness to formation of the cores in our solar system.

So, it my belief the bottomless may have this meaning a period when the cores are formed? Also, they are speaking on our solar system in Enoch 27 and 28 and the formations of cores which froze over. This also agrees with what those of the University of Liverpool are saying.

THIRD DAY

SCIENCE

(4.6 billion years ago)

As Earth cooled, an atmosphere formed mainly from gases spewed from volcanoes. It included hydrogen sulfide, methane, and ten to 200 times as much carbon dioxide as today's atmosphere.

"And God said, let there be a firmament in the midst of the waters, and let it divide the waters from the waters. And God made the firmament, and divided the waters which were under the firmament from the waters which were above the firmament: and it was so.

And God called the firmament Heaven. And the evening and the morning were the second day."
Genesis 1:6-8 KJV

FOURTH DAY

So, on about the second day the atmosphere forms as land mass forms as also do the books of God say.

SCIENCE

The sun formed **more than 4.5 billion years ago**, when a cloud of dust and gas called a nebula collapsed under its own gravity. As it did, the cloud spun and flattened into a disk, with our sun forming at its center. The disk's outskirts later accreted into our solar system, including Earth and the other planets.

So, the Sun would have not been bright due the ring of gas and clouds around the sun.

SCIENCE

After **between three and ten million years**, the young Sun's solar wind would have cleared away all the gas and dust in the protoplanetary disc, blowing it into interstellar space, thus ending the growth of the planets.

Enoch 26

AND I summoned the very lowest a second time, and said: 'Let Archas come forth hard,' and he came forth hard from the invisible.

2 And Archas came forth, hard, heavy, and very red.

3 And I said: 'Be opened, Archas, and let there be born from thee,' and he came undone, an age came forth, very great and very dark, bearing the creation of all lower things, and I saw that it was good and said to him:

4 'Go thou down below, and make thyself firm, and be for a foundation for the lower things,' and it happened and he went down and fixed himself, and became the foundation for the lower things, and below the darkness there is nothing else.

"And God saw the light, that it was good: and God divided the light from the darkness. And God called the light Day, and the darkness he called Night. And the evening and the morning were the first day."
Genesis 1:4-5 KJV

SCIENCE

How long was the light and darkness of big bang

The fog didn't lift until 1 billion years after the Big Bang, when the neutral hydrogen had been reionized and once again split apart. Because light couldn't escape its surroundings during the dark ages, it couldn't journey outward through the universe to hit our detectors here on Earth, nearly 13 billion years later.

So, the period scientists and science are saying the 1 day of God is is a billion years. So, I think due to time travel it's impossible to know the time frame. But God Archas immediately fixed himself after being created. So, it should be consistent from then until now. That we as sons of God might determine, if of God.

What does God say about the darkness? You notice science calls it a cosmic dark age. Enoch says in 26 and 3 an age came forth, very great and very dark bearing the creation of lower things.

And God said, Let the earth bring forth grass, the herb yielding seed, and the fruit tree yielding fruit after his kind, whose seed is, upon the earth: and it was so. And the earth brought forth grass, and herb yielding seed after his kind, and the tree yielding fruit, whose seed was in itself, after his kind: and God saw that it was good. And the evening and the morning were the third day."
Genesis 1:11-13 KJV

THE GARDEN IS ENCLOSED AND LIT, ADAM NEVER SAW THE SUN

GOD

Secrets of Enoch 30

ON the third day I commanded the earth to make grow great and fruitful trees, and hills, and seed to sow, and I planted Paradise, and enclosed it, and placed as armed guardians flaming angels, and thus I created renewal.

1st Book Adam and Eve 1

ON the third day, God planted the garden in the east of the earth, on the border of the world eastward, beyond which, towards the sun-rising, one finds nothing but water, that encompasses the whole world, and reaches unto the borders of heaven.

I won't talk about renewal right now that's a whole subject in itself.

1st Book of Adam and Eve 12: 7, 8, 9, 10

7 Then Adam arose in the cave and said, "O God, wherefore has light departed from us, and darkness come over us? Wherefore dost Thou leave us in this long darkness? Why wilt Thou plague us thus?
8 "And this darkness, O Lord, where was it ere it came upon us? It is such, that we cannot see each other.

SCIENCE

Plant life

New data and analysis show that plant life began colonizing land 500 million years ago, during the Cambrian Period, around the same time as the emergence of the first land animals

SCIENCE

The Earth formed over 4.6 billion years ago out of a mixture of dust and gas around the young sun. It grew larger thanks to countless collisions between dust particles, asteroids, and other growing planets, including one last giant impact that threw enough rock, gas, and dust into space to form the moon.

In timely news, scientists have determined that some 1.4 billion years ago, an Earth day—that is, a full rotation around its axis—took 18 hours and 41 minutes, rather than the familiar 24 hours, The Guardian reports. According to new calculations published in the Proceedings of the National Academy of Sciences, Earth adds an average of .0000135 seconds to the length of its day every year, a trend that is on track to continue for millions of years more. Researchers came to their conclusion about Earth's deep time while looking in ancient sediment deposits for markers of climate change related to periodic variations in the planet's orbit .

I guess the point is man was not put into the garden until we had a 24-hour day. So, and that Adam never saw the sun until put out of the Garden, that Adam never saw darkness until put out of the Garden. Fact is the garden could have been in a ship for all we know. Who knows what renewal encompasses. Further Satan had an alien race here which may go back to the earth's core.

Bearing
noun
bear·ing ˈber-iŋ
2
a
: the act, power, or time of bringing forth offspring or fruit
a woman past bearing
b
: a product of bearing : CROP
three bearings in a year
3
a
: an object, surface, or point that supports

GOD

9 "For, so long as we were in the garden, we neither saw nor even knew what darkness is. I was not hidden from Eve, neither was she hidden from me, until now that she cannot see me; and no darkness came upon us, to separate us from each other.

10 "But she and I were both in one bright light. I saw her and she saw me. Yet now since we came into this cave, darkness has come upon us, and parted us asunder, so that I do not see her, and she does not see me.

en·clo·sure

/enˈklōZHər,inˈklōZHər/

1. an area that is sealed off with an artificial or natural barrier.
2. the state of being enclosed,

1st Book of Adam and Eve 16:6, 7

6 For he thought the sun was God.

7 Inasmuch as while he was in the garden and heard the voice of God and the sound He made in the garden, and feared Him, Adam never saw the brilliant light of the sun, neither did the flaming heat thereof touch his body.

Point: Adam was in the garden 7 years and never saw the sun because it was enclosed

2: Adam and Eve glowed bright, as many will after resurrection.

3: they'll be many to say what it isn't, but none to say what it is. And you can't have it both ways.

1st Book of Adam and Eve 11

6 And she said unto him, "Lo, I am standing in this darkness."

7 He then said to her, "Remember the bright nature in which we lived, while we abode in the garden!

8 "O Eve! remember the glory that rested on us in the garden. O Eve! remember the trees that overshadowed us in the garden while we moved among them.

17 And after the completion of the seven years, which he had completed there, seven years exactly, and in the second month, on the seventeenth
day the serpent came and approached the woman, and the serpent said to the woman, "Hath God commanded you, saying, Ye shall not eat of every tree of the garden?"

26 And He made for them coats of skin, and clothed them, and sent them forth from the Garden of Eden.

27. And on that day on which Adam went forth from the garden, he offered as a sweet savour an offering, frankincense, galbanum, and stacte, and spices in the morning with the rising of the sun from the day when he covered his shame.

28 And on that day was closed the mouth of all beasts, and of cattle, and of birds, and of whatever walketh, and of whatever moveth, so that they could no longer speak: for they had all spoken one with another with one lip and with one tongue.

29 And He sent out of the Garden of Eden all flesh that was in the Garden of Eden, and all flesh was scattered according to its kinds, and according to its types unto the places which had been created for them.

30 And to Adam alone did He give (the wherewithal) to cover his shame, of all the beasts and cattle.

31 On this account, it is prescribed on the heavenly tables as touching all those who know the judgment of the law, that they should cover their shame, and should not uncover themselves as the Gentiles uncover themselves.

32 And on the new moon of the fourth month, Adam and his wife went forth from the Garden

So, let's look at the atmosphere, which was forming in the second day, along with land mass water. Here's the thing they start talking about these thousand years periods, not so much about the creation, because I'm pretty sure time was stuck together during the creation to accelerate the process of the creation.

ON the third day I commanded the earth to make grow great and fruitful trees, and hills, and seed to sow, and I planted Paradise, and enclosed it, and placed as armed guardians flaming angels, and thus I created renewal.

This is evidence that the garden was an enclosure and covered. With Adam never had seen the sun before. This evidence is to show that the garden is older than what scientists and science say the earth could grow food. The garden is a controlled environment and Adam testimony is combined with Enochs.

Now this is as late as sixth day! So, the seventh day could be a thousand years. I have contradicted science with evidence the garden was in closed. And for how many years did they study renewal?

re·new·al
/rəˈnooəl/
 Learn to pronounce
noun
an instance of resuming an activity or state after an interruption.

Evolution and renewal have almost the same meaning.

ev·o·lu·tion
/ˌevəˈlooSH(ə)n/
 Learn to pronounce
See definitions in:
All
Biology
Chemistry
Military
Mathematics · Dated
noun
1.the process by which different kinds of living organisms are thought to have developed and diversified from earlier forms during the history of the earth.

Jubilees 23

26 And in those days the children will begin to study the laws, and to seek the commandments, And to return to the path of righteousness.

27 And the days will begin to grow many and increase amongst those children of men, Till their days draw nigh to one thousand years, and to a greater number of years than (before) was the number of the days.

28 And there will be no old man nor one who is not satisfied with his days, For all will be (as) children and youths.

29 And all their days they will complete and live in peace and in joy, and there will be no Satan nor any evil destroyer; For all their days will be days of blessing and healing,

30 And at that time the Lord will heal His servants, and they will rise up and see great peace, And drive out their adversaries And the righteous will see and be thankful, And rejoice with joy for ever and ever, And will see all their judgments and all their curses on their enemies.

31 And their bones will rest in the earth, and their spirits will have much joy, they will enjoy a blessed immortality And they will know that it is the Lord who executeth judgment, And showeth mercy to hundreds and thousands and to all that love Him.

32 And do thou, Moses, write down these words; for thus are they written, and they record (them) on the heavenly tables for a testimony for the generations forever.

1st Book of Adam and Eve

6 And the Word of God came unto Adam and raised him from his death and opened Eve's mouth that she might speak.

7 Then Adam arose in the cave and said, "O God, wherefore has light departed from us, and darkness come over us? Wherefore dost Thou leave us in this long darkness? Why wilt Thou plague us thus?

8 "And this darkness, O Lord, where was it ere it came upon us? It is such, that we cannot see each other.

9 "For, so long as we were in the garden, we neither saw nor even knew what darkness is. I was not hidden from Eve, neither was she hidden from me, until now that she cannot see me; and no darkness came upon us, to separate us from each other.

10 "But she and I were both in one bright light. I saw her and she saw me. Yet now since we came into this cave, darkness has come upon us, and parted us asunder, so that I do not see her, and she does not see me.

So, Adam had never saw night or the sun, while in the garden. Which means it was lit and covered as a enclosure. And here Adam himself is saying it. You see they knew the importance of this information in proving they are originally from earth in flesh. But the spirit that's in man where is that derived from? Since also the garden is an enclosed structure.

1st Book of Adam and Eve 16
6 For he thought the sun was God.
7 Inasmuch as while he was in the garden and heard the voice of God and the sound He made in the garden, and feared Him, Adam never saw the brilliant light of the sun, neither did the flaming heat thereof touch his body.

enclosed
/inˈklōzd,enˈklōzd/
Learn to pronounce
See definitions in:
All
Religion
Farming
Mathematics
adjective
surrounded or closed off on all sides.
Enclosure
: the act or action of enclosing: the quality or state of being enclosed. :

1st Book of Adam and Eve 11

6 And she said unto him, "Lo, I am standing in this darkness."

7 He then said to her, "Remember the bright nature in which we lived, while we abode in the garden!

8 "O Eve! remember the glory that rested on us in the garden. O Eve! remember the trees that overshadowed us in the garden while we moved among them.

17 And after the completion of the seven years, which he had completed there, seven years exactly, and in the second month, on the seventeenth

day the serpent came and approached the woman, and the serpent said to the woman, "Hath God commanded you, saying, Ye shall not eat of every tree of the garden?"

26 And He made for them coats of skin, and clothed them, and sent them forth from the Garden of Eden.

27 And on that day on which Adam went forth from the garden, he offered as a sweet savour an offering, frankincense, galbanum, and stacte, and spices in the morning with the rising of the sun from the day when he covered his shame.

28 And on that day was closed the mouth of all beasts, and of cattle, and of birds, and of whatever walketh, and of whatever moveth, so that they could no longer speak: for they had all spoken one with another with one lip and with one tongue.

29 And He sent out of the Garden of Eden all flesh that was in the Garden of Eden, and all flesh was scattered according to its kinds, and according to its types unto the places which had been created for them.

30 And to Adam alone did He give (the wherewithal) to cover his shame, of all the beasts and cattle.

31 On this account, it is prescribed on the heavenly tables as touching all those who know the judgment of the law, that they should cover their shame, and should not uncover themselves as the Gentiles uncover themselves.

32 And on the new moon of the fourth month, Adam and his wife went forth from the Garden

EPIGRAPH

What is the woman?

"And there appeared a great wonder in heaven; a woman clothed with the sun, and the moon under her feet, and upon her head a crown of twelve stars:"
Revelation 12:1 KJV

Revelation 12:1 partial interpretation of the 12 stars from the war in Heaven
Addendum
Clothed with the sun meaning.
- if the clothing means the sun is seven times brighter, then the resurrection is taking place.

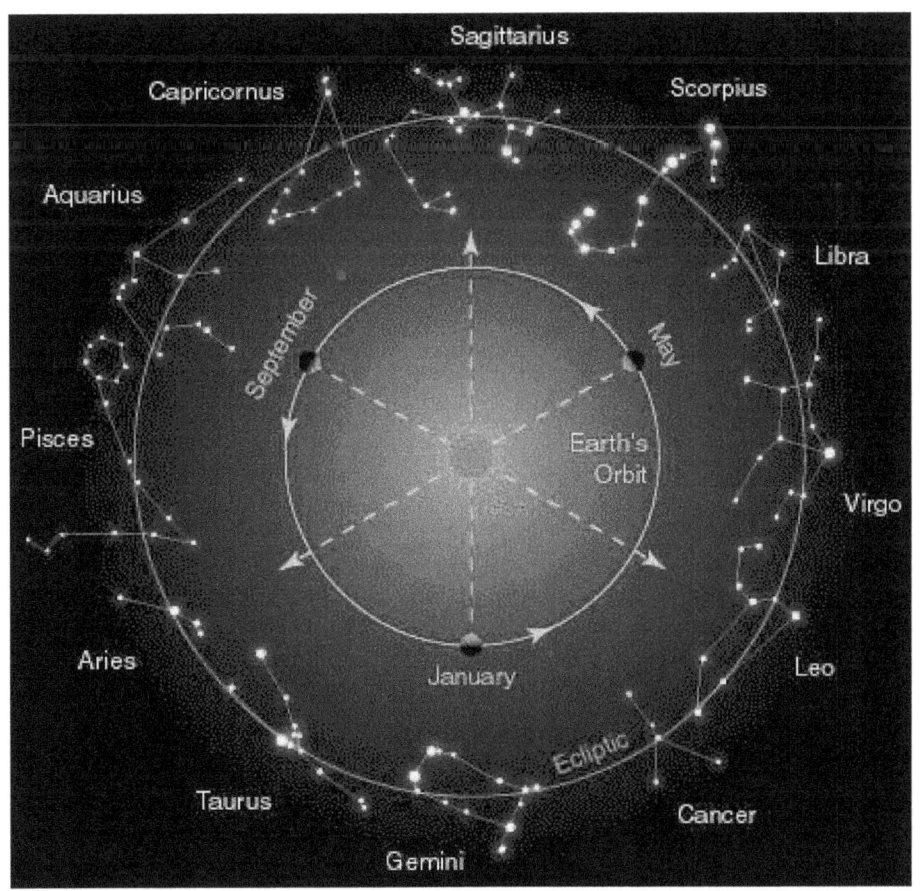

CHAPTER 12
WAR IN HEAVEN

Before there Time Arrived is a deep meaning.

If it's man if they go back before there time arrived, it means before being created.

But it's probably not man but other alien races who came to earth sooner than they should, Satan was black in fact

16 The stars which roll over fire are those which transgressed the commandment of God before their time arrived; for they came not in their proper season. Therefore, was He offended with them, and bound them, until the period of the consummation of their crimes in the secret year.
Note there was life here on earth such as angel life both good and bad when Adam was created. The fallen angels are here, and they appear to go back to the bottomless or second day, though their world may not have been created till the fifth day. So, it still looks like time travel. And remember they fell before their time came. They came before they should, but it still adds up to time travel.

And certainly, rather than through time travel and attrition did those angels propose to fight God. Only faithless men propose the fallen angels are the sons of Seth, removing books only to be able to say what you say outside the actual teaching.

Adam and Eve 13
15 "But thou didst not keep one day My commandment; until I had finished the creation and blessed everything in it.
16 "Then I commanded thee concerning the tree, that thou eat not thereof. Yet I knew that Satan, who deceived himself, would also deceive thee.

17 "So I made known to thee by means of the tree, not to come near him. And I told thee not to eat of the fruit thereof, nor to taste of it, nor yet to sit under it, nor to yield to it.

Secrets of Enoch 28

Those men took me on to the fifth heaven and placed me, and there I saw many and countless soldiers, called Grigori, of human appearance, and their size was greater than that of great giants and their faces withered, and the silence of their mouth's perpetual, and there was no service on the fifth heaven, and I said to the men who were with me:

2 Wherefore are these very withered and their faces melancholy, and their mouths silent, and wherefore is there no service on this heaven?

3 And they said to me: These are the Grigori, who with their prince Satanail rejected the Lord of light, and after them are those who are held in great darkness on the second heaven, and three of them went down on to earth from the Lord's throne, to the place Ermon, and broke through their vows on the shoulder of the hill Ermon and saw the daughters of men how good they are, and took to themselves wives, and befouled the earth with their deeds, who in all times of their age made lawlessness and mixing, and giants are born and marvelous big men and great enmity.

4 And therefore God judged them with great judgement, and they weep for their brethren and they will be punished on the Lord's great day.

5 And I said to the Grigori: 'I saw your brethren and their works, and their great torments, and I prayed for them, but the Lord has condemned them to be under earth till heaven and earth shall end forever.

Secrets of Enoch 29

AND for all the heavenly troops I imaged the image and essence of fire, and my eye looked at the very hard, firm rock, and from the gleam of my eye the lightning received its wonderful nature, which is both fire in water and water in fire, and one does not put out the other, nor does the one dry up the other, therefore the lightning is brighter than the sun, softer than water and firmer than hard rock.

2 And from the rock I cut off a great fire, and from the fire I created the orders of the incorporeal ten troops of angels, and their weapons are fiery and their raiment a burning flame, and I commanded that each one should stand in his order.

Here Satanail with his angels was thrown down from the height.

Enoch 85

1 Again I looked attentively, 1 while sleeping, and surveyed heaven above.

2 And behold a single star fell from heaven.

3 Which being raised up, ate and fed among those cows.

Secrets of Enoch

3 And one from out the order of angels, having turned away with the order that was under him, conceived an impossible thought, to place his throne higher than the clouds above the earth, that he might become equal in rank to my power.

4 And I threw him out from the height with his angels, and he was flying in the air continuously above the bottomless.

Secrets of Enoch 28

AND then I made firm the heavenly circle, and made that the lower water which is under heaven collect itself together, into one whole, and that the chaos become dry, and it became so.

2 Out of the waves I created rock hard and big, and from the rock I piled up the dry, and the dry I called earth, and the midst of the earth I called abyss, that is to say the bottomless, I collected the sea in one place and bound it together with a yoke.

3 And I said to the sea: 'Behold I give thee thy eternal limits, and thou shalt not break loose from thy component parts.'

4 Thus I made fast the firmament. This day I called me the first-created.

Now verse four of Secrets of Enoch appear to be tampered with, by those who seek to discredit the book. And certainly, men are capable of such.

I have heard many in the Church say that God spirit was in them when they removed the books of God. And said God would not allow them to make such a mistake to mislead all the generations of the earth after Christ.

But they speak proudly about something they cannot prove. Even when Gods word came to Adam, who misled all the generations of the earth by his sin. God told Adam 13:18 it would have been an offence on My part, for not having given thee any order; thou wouldst turn round and blame Me for it.

So, please don't put your words in the mouth of God, you are much like Satan in 1st Book Adam and Eve 13:16 Yet I knew that Satan, who deceived himself. So, in fact you are deceiving yourselves as also did Satan deceive himself. You are very capable of misleading the earth in truth and have done so.

1st book Adam and Eve 13
14 "For I made thee of the light; and I willed to bring out children of light from thee and like unto thee.
15 "But thou didst not keep one day My commandment; until I had finished the creation and blessed everything in it.
16 "Then I commanded thee concerning the tree, that thou eat not thereof. Yet I knew that Satan, who deceived himself, would also deceive thee.
17 "So I made known to thee by means of the tree, not to come near him. And I told thee not to eat of the fruit thereof, nor to taste of it, nor yet to sit under it, nor to yield to it.
18 "Had I not been and spoken to thee, O Adam, concerning the tree, and had I left thee without a commandment, and thou hadst sinned--it would have been an offence on My part, for not having given thee any order; thou wouldst turn round and blame Me for it.
19 "But I commanded thee, and warned thee, and thou didst fall. So that My creatures cannot blame me; but the blame rests on them alone.

Adam and Eve 6
3 He, therefore, sent His Word unto them; that they should stand and be raised forthwith.

4 And the Lord said unto Adam and Eve, "You transgressed of your own free will, until you came out of the garden in which I had placed you.

5 "Of your own free will have you transgressed through your desire for divinity, greatness, and an exalted state, such as I have; so that I deprived you of the bright nature in which you then were, and I made you come out of the garden to this land, rough and full of trouble.

6 "If only you had not transgressed My commandment and had kept My law and had not eaten of the fruit of the tree, near which I told you not to come! And there were fruit trees in the garden better than that one.

7 "But the wicked Satan who continued not in his first estate, nor kept his faith; in whom was no good intent towards Me, and who though I had created him, yet set Me at naught, and sought the Godhead, so that I hurled him down from heaven,--he it is who made the tree appear pleasant in your eyes, until you ate of it, by hearkening to him.

8 "Thus have you transgressed My commandment, and therefore have I brought upon you all these sorrows.

PROPHECY

It's my belief a near Moneyless System is established in the early days of the resurrection. A thousand years of peace with Christ is come.

MONEYLESS SYSTEM

"And when he had opened the third seal, I heard the third beast say, Come and see. And I beheld, and lo a black horse; and he that sat on him had a pair of balances in his hand. And I heard a voice in the midst of the four beasts say, A measure of wheat for a penny, and three measures of barley for a penny; and see thou hurt not the oil and the wine."

Revelation 6:5-6 KJV

TOWARDS THE END 1000 YEARS OF RESURRECTION

At the end of the thousand Satan is loosed. The Monetary System appears to be trying to get re-established. These are those which fight God.

SOME ANGELIC EVIL RESURRECTED

"And I beheld another beast coming up out of the earth; and he had two horns like a lamb, and he spake as a dragon. And he exerciseth all the power of the first beast before him, and causeth the earth and them which dwell therein to worship the first beast, whose deadly wound was healed. And he doeth great wonders, so that he maketh fire come down from heaven on the earth in the sight of men,"
Revelation 13:11-13 KJV

SATAN AND THE FALLEN ANGELS TIME JUMPED

2 And behold a single star fell from heaven.
3 Which being raised up, ate and fed among those cows.

Enoch 85
2 And behold a single star fell from heaven.
3 Which being raised up, ate and fed among those cows.
4 After that I perceived other large and black cows; and behold all of them changed their stalls and pastures, while their young began to lament one with another. Again, I looked in my vision, and surveyed heaven; when behold I saw many stars which descended, and projected themselves from heaven to where the first star was,

FALLEN ANGELS JUMP BACK IN TIME

3 And they said to me: These are the Grigori, who with their prince Satanail rejected the Lord of light, and after them are those who are held in great darkness on the second heaven, and three of them went down on to earth from the Lord's throne, to the place Ermon, and broke through their vows on the shoulder of the hill Ermon

TIME TRAVEL

- Lords throne not yet built.

1 - Fallen Angels already came.

2- Throne not yet built so it's Evidence they are from the future. A place not yet come into existence.

3- Throne built sometime in the next millennium up to 1500 years from now.

NOTE SATAN IS BLACK

4 After that I perceived other large and black cows; and behold all of them changed their stalls and pastures, while their young began to lament one with another. Again I looked in my vision, and surveyed heaven; when behold I saw many stars which descended, and projected themselves from heaven to where the first star was,

1st Book of Adam and Eve
4 And look, O Adam, at him, who said of himself that he is God! Can God be black? Would God take the form of a woman? Is there any one stronger than God? And can He be overpowered?

Secrets of Enoch 7
AND those men took me and led me up on to the second heaven, and showed me darkness, greater than earthly darkness, and there I saw prisoners hanging, watched, awaiting the great and

boundless judgement, and these angels were dark-looking, more than earthly darkness, and incessantly making weeping through all hours.

Secrets of Enoch 18

3 And they said to me: These are the Grigori, who with their prince Satanail rejected the Lord of light, and after them are those who are held in great darkness on the second heaven, and three of them went down on to earth from the Lord's throne, to the place Ermon, and broke through their vows on the shoulder of the hill Ermon

MONETARY SYSTEM RE-ESTABLISHED

"And he causeth all, both small and great, rich and poor, free and bond, to receive a mark in their right hand, or in their foreheads: and that no man might buy or sell, save he that had the mark, or the name of the beast, or the number of his name."
Revelation 13:16-17 KJV

"And it shall be, as with the people, so with the priest; as with the servant, so with his master; as with the maid, so with her mistress; as with the buyer, so with the seller; as with the lender, so with the borrower; as with the taker of usury, so with the giver of usury to him."
Isaiah 24:2 KJV

CAUSING THE BATTLE OF ARMAGEDDON

"Therefore, hath the curse devoured the earth, and they that dwell therein are desolate: therefore, the inhabitants of the earth are burned, and few men left."
Isaiah 24:6 KJV

"And they went up on the breadth of the earth, and compassed the camp of the saints about, and the beloved city: and fire came down from God out of heaven and devoured them."
Revelation 20:9 KJV

QUESTION OF THE SEVENTY ANGELS

As for these? It's a question? But, to me it seems many Gods sprang up around the world about the "Time Tower of Babel Fell."

1- pyramid structures appear around the world from that time, and many God.

The Question Is? Are these the teachings of the 70 angels which God will judge. (After The Flood) Note: this does not mean all pyramids are made after the flood. But those made after the flood may have originated with the 70 angels?

Jasher 9

32 And God said to the seventy angels who stood foremost before him, to those who were near to him, saying, Come let us descend and confuse their tongues, that one man shall not understand the language of his neighbor, and they did so unto them.

Enoch 89

30 Upon this sat the Lord of the sheep, who received all the sealed books.

31 Which were open before him.

32 Then the Lord called the first seven white ones and commanded them to bring before him the first of the first stars, which preceded the stars whose form partly resembled that of horses; the first star, which fell down first; and they brought them all before him.

33 And he spoke to the man who wrote in his presence, who was one of the seven white ones, saying, Take those seventy shepherds, to whom I delivered up the sheep, and who receiving them killed more of them than I commanded.

REVELATION 12 THE WAR IN HEAVEN

"And there appeared a great wonder in heaven; a woman clothed with the sun, and the moon under her feet, and upon her head a crown of twelve stars:"

Revelation 12:1 KJV

Secrets of Enoch 30

The true meaning and the interpretation of the War in Heaven. This verse picks up on the fourth day. And about the time the sun and stars are created.

Enoch 27
But this sounds more like Michael the Archangel rather than Christ. Who, do you know in the Bible who comes from the North. When most all are in the east. Further these things happen after the resurrection.

"I have raised up one from the north, and he shall come: from the rising of the sun shall he call upon my name: and he shall come upon princes as upon morter, and as the potter treadeth clay.

Who hath declared from the beginning, that we may know? and beforetime, that we may say, He is righteous? yea, there is none that sheweth, yea, there is none that declareth, yea, there is none that heareth your words."
Isaiah 41:25-26 KJV

"And he that overcometh, and keepeth my works unto the end, to him will I give power over the nations: And he shall rule them with a rod of iron; as the vessels of a potter shall they be broken to shivers: even as I received of my Father."
Revelation 2:26-27 KJV

Enoch 20
5 Michael, one of the holy angels, who, presiding over human virtue, commands the nations.

You see Revelation 2: 27 even as I received of my Father. And that's Christ talking about another man than himself. And who is this man written about from before the flood who is not Christ. And whom Christ himself also speaks?

"To him that overcometh will I grant to sit with me in my throne, even as I also overcame, and am set down with my Father in his throne."

Revelation 3:21 KJV

"And he that overcometh, and keepeth my works unto the end, to him will I give power over the nations:"

Revelation 2:26 KJV

This star is capable of time travel, I guess the importance of it is, how far back did it go. The Bottomless is created the first and second day. Seemingly the cores of planets.

Fact is on the fifth day; God made the stars. Unlike you all, I cannot see these as twenty-four hour periods. I think though Time Travel is possible God fixed Time, but when in the creation did he do it? That would matter in trying to understand creation and the length of time taken to create all things. Or was time altered then fixed?

Esdras 4:

37 By measure hath he measured the times; and by number hath he numbered the times; and he doth not move nor stir them, until the said measure be fulfilled.

So, Esdras 4:37 is saying Time is Consistent until a certain period. This period of Time Travel is also implying where God comes from. So, if Time Travel isn't started until our future, it points a finger at who and where God came from.

So, the fact would be Time is fixed until it's broken 13 or 14 billion years after creation. Though God jumped back or forward in Time, time would remain fixed until broken in about 480 years from now more or less. But this does not say, time was always fixed, it leaves a question about just what is fixed in time. Maybe just the time where stuck in is fixed? Looks like at least time may be calibrated for a particular period.

Enoch 81

8. Truly has been stated, and accurately has been computed that which is marked down; for the luminaries, the months, the fixed periods, the years, and the days, Uriel has explained to me, and communicated to me; whom the Lord of all creation, on my account, commanded (according to

the might of heaven, and the power which it possesses both by night and by day) to explain the laws of light to man, of the sun, moon, and stars, and of all the powers of heaven, which are turned with their respective orbs.

9 This is the ordinance of the stars, which set in their places, in their seasons, in their periods, in their days, and in their months.

So, by these writings it appears Time is fixed which aids in our learning the creation and making science and calculations possible in all things. Which might also aid in the discovery of Time Travel by our learning.

Set 1

AND I commanded that there should be taken from light and darkness, and I said: 'Be thick,' and it became thus and I spread it out with the light, and it became water, and I spread it out over the darkness, below the light, and then I made firm the waters, that is to say the bottomless, and I made foundation of light around the water, and created seven circles from inside, and imaged it (sc. the water) like crystal wet and dry, that is to say like glass, and the circumcession of the waters and the other elements, and I showed each one of them its road, and the seven stars each one of them in its heaven, that they go thus, and I saw that it was good.

Enoch 30

4 On the first uppermost circle I placed the stars, Kruno, and on the second Aphrodit, on the third Aris, on the fifth Zeus, on the sixth Ermis, on the seventh lesser the moon, and adorned it with the lesser stars

5 And on the lower I placed the sun for the illumination of day, and the moon and stars for the illumination of night.

6 The sun that it should go according to each animal (sc. signs of the zodiac), twelve, and I appointed the succession of the months and their names and lives, their thunderings, and their hour-markings, how they should succeed.

"And I beheld when he had opened the sixth seal, and, lo, there was a great earthquake; and the sun became black as sackcloth of hair, and the moon became as blood;"

Revelation 6:12 KJV

And the stars of heaven fell unto the earth, even as a fig tree casteth her untimely figs, when she is shaken of a mighty wind. And the heaven departed as a scroll when it is rolled together; and every mountain and island were moved out of their places.

Revelation 6:13-14 KJV

Enoch 29

AND for all the heavenly troops I imaged the image and essence of fire, and my eye looked at the very hard, firm rock, and from the gleam of my eye the lightning received its wonderful nature, which is both fire in water and water in fire, and one does not put out the other, nor does the one dry up the other, therefore the lightning is brighter than the sun, softer than water and firmer than hard rock.

2 And from the rock I cut off a great fire, and from the fire I created the orders of the incorporeal ten troops of angels, and their weapons are fiery and their raiment a burning flame, and I commanded that each one should stand in his order.

Here Satanail with his angels was thrown down from the height.

3 And one from out the order of angels, having turned away with the order that was under him, conceived an impossible thought, to place his throne higher than the clouds above the earth, that he might become equal in rank to my power.

4 And I threw him out from the height with his angels, and he was flying in the air continuously above the bottomless.

Now at this point, it appears to be after the resurrection when the angels become angels. So, it's extremely hard to determine. But, without knowing I must try and understand. So, I will try and piece together.

"And there appeared another wonder in heaven; and behold a great red dragon, having seven heads and ten horns, and seven crowns upon his heads. And his tail drew the third part of the stars of heaven, and did cast them to the earth: and the dragon stood before the woman, which was ready to be delivered, for to devour her child as soon as it was born."

Revelation 12:3-4 KJV

Secrets of Enoch 20

AND those two men lifted me up thence on to the seventh Heaven, and I saw there a very great light, and fiery troops of great archangels, incorporeal forces, and dominions, orders and governments, cherubim and seraphim, thrones and many-eyed ones, nine regiments, the Ioanit stations of light, and I became afraid, and began to tremble with great terror, and those men took me, and led me after them, and said to me:

2 'Have courage, Enoch, do not fear,' and showed me the Lord from afar, sitting on His very high throne. For what is there on the tenth heaven, since the Lord dwells here?

3 On the tenth heaven is God, in the Hebrew tongue he is called Aravat.

4 And all the heavenly troops would come and stand on the ten steps according to their rank, and would bow down to the Lord, and would again go to their places in joy and felicity, singing songs in the boundless light with small and tender voices, gloriously serving him.

Secrets of Enoch 23

AND for all the heavenly troops I imaged the image and essence of fire, and my eye looked at the very hard, firm rock, and from the gleam of my eye the lightning received its wonderful nature, which is both fire in water and water in fire, and one does not put out the other, nor does the one dry up the other, therefore the lightning is brighter than the sun, softer than water and firmer than hard rock.

2 And from the rock I cut off a great fire, and from the fire I created the orders of the incorporeal ten troops of angels, and their weapons are fiery and their raiment a burning flame, and I commanded that each one should stand in his order.

3 And one from out the order of angels, having turned away with the order that was under him, conceived an impossible thought, to place his throne higher than the clouds above the earth, that he might become equal in rank to my power.

4 And I threw him out from the height with his angels, and he was flying in the air continuously above the bottomless.

At this point I see the seven stars as perhaps the seven worlds created and the Ten Horn are the Ten Ranks of Incorporeal Troops of God. They perhaps are spread out over the seven stars. But those at Jupiter with his host turned on God.

Secrets of Enoch 18

THE men took me on to the fifth heaven and placed me, and there I saw many and countless soldiers, called Grigori, of human appearance, and their size was greater than that of great giants and their faces withered, and the silence of their mouth's perpetual, and there was no service on the fifth heaven, and I said to the men who were with me:

2 Wherefore are these very withered and their faces melancholy, and their mouths silent, and wherefore is there no service on this heaven?

3 And they said to me: These are the Grigori, who with their prince Satanail rejected the Lord of light, and after them are those who are held in great darkness on the second heaven, and three of them went down on to earth from the Lord's throne, to the place Ermon, and broke through their vows on the shoulder of the hill Ermon and saw the daughters of men how good they are, and took to themselves wives, and befouled the earth with their deeds, who in all times of their age made lawlessness and mixing, and giants are born and marvelous big men and great enmity.

So, here is where it's written they are black, many talk about black being on earth before Adam. Yes, probably, but what is the context of them being here. Nor does it mean God was not working on renewal before man was created. And or that other angels were not created on earth prior to man.

Recall plant life may have existed on earth about 200 million years before dinosaurs or mammals. So, I wonder what was going on in those days. But what is written the dragon was here on earth prior to man. Or prior to the resurrection of man and Christ being put on the throne. So, perhaps that's another reason Christ was raised early, because of something which happened in the end.

Secrets of Enoch 7

AND those men took me and led me up on to the second heaven, and showed me darkness, greater than earthly darkness, and there I saw prisoners hanging, watched, awaiting the great and

boundless judgement, and these angels were **dark-looking, more than earthly darkness**, and incessantly making weeping through all hours.

2 And I said to the men who were with me: 'Wherefore are these incessantly tortured?' they answered me: 'These are God's apostates, who obeyed not God's commands, but took counsel with their own will, and turned away with their prince, who also is fastened on the fifth heaven.'

The Second Book of Adam and Eve 4

4 And look, O Adam, at him, who said of himself that he is God! **Can God be black?** Would God take the form of a woman? Is there any one stronger than God? And can He be overpowered?

"For where two or three are gathered together in my name, there am I in the midst of them."
Matthew 18:20 KJV

So, with two books saying Satan is Black, gives me the authority to teach Satan was blacker than those of earth according to the teaching.

And recall, I said I went up into a ship a UFO which stood over a street in a vision. In which one tried to cut me in a fight, in reality. Going inside that ship I saw a pitch-black angel who attempted to pray for me over that place.

But he spoke as a Telepathic and his voice was heard but his mouth did not move. He tried to shake my hand after he finished to pray. But when I did not shake his hand he yelled at me Amen, loud and angry. I then left him where I saw many of the great men of earth history held there in that place. Pleading to me not to follow that angel or shake his hand.

Enoch 89
29 And I saw a throne erected in a delectable land.
30 Upon this sat the Lord of the sheep, who received all the sealed books.

Secrets of Enoch 18

3 And they said to me: These are the Grigori, who with their prince Satanail rejected the Lord of light, and after them are those who are held in great darkness on the second heaven, **and three of them went down on to earth from the Lord's throne,** to the place Ermon, and broke through their vows on the shoulder of the hill Ermon and saw the daughters of men how good they are, and took to themselves wives, and befouled the earth with their deeds, who in all times of their age made lawlessness and mixing, and giants are born and marvellous big men and great enmity.

1st Book of Adam and Eve 55

8 "But now, O Adam, we will make known to thee, what came upon us through him, before his fall from heaven.

9 "He gathered together his hosts, and deceived them, promising them to give them a great kingdom, a divine nature; and other promises he made them.

10 "His hosts believed that. his word was true, so they yielded to him, and renounced the glory of God.

11 "He then sent for us according to the orders in which we were-to come under his command, and to hearken to his vain promise. But we would not, and we took not his advice.

12 "Then after he had fought with God, and had dealt forwardly with Him, he gathered together his hosts, and made war with us. And if it had not been for God's strength that was with us, we could not have prevailed against him to hurl him from heaven.

13 "But when he fell from among us, there was great joy in heaven, because of his going down from us. For had he continued in heaven, nothing, not even one angel would have remained in it.

14 "But God in His mercy, drove him from among us to this dark earth; for he had become darkness itself and a worker of unrighteousness.

15 "And he has continued, O Adam, to make war against thee, until he beguiled thee and made thee come out of the garden, to this strange land, where all these trials have come to thee.

Enoch 85

2 And behold a single star fell from heaven.

3 Which being raised up, ate and fed among those cows.

4 (partial) Again I looked in my vision, and surveyed heaven; when behold I saw many stars which descended, and projected themselves from heaven to where the first star was

Enoch 18

And death, which God brought upon him he has also brought to thee, O Adam, because thou didst obey him, and didst transgress against God."

16 Then the angels rejoiced and praised God, and asked Him not to destroy Adam this time, for his having sought to enter the garden; but to bear with him until the fulfilment of the promise; and to help him in this world until he was free from Satan's hand.

TIME TRAVEL BACK IN TIME CRIME

So, the point is once the throne gets built, and you have three Grigori come down. Back in time from the end to the beginning. These are those who fell before their time arrived. So, to go to any earlier period and then try and change time it's much like what Daniel teaches. To go back in Time and stop even Christ from being born. To bread man out, to overthrow God.

16 The stars which roll over fire are those which transgressed the commandment of God before their time arrived; for they came not in their proper season. Therefore, was He offended with them, and bound them, until the period of the consummation of their crimes in the secret year.

Enoch 89
29 And I saw a throne erected in a delectable land.
30 Upon this sat the Lord of the sheep, who received all the sealed books.
32 Then the Lord called the first seven white ones, and commanded them to bring before him the first of the first stars,

"Until the Ancient of days came, and judgment was given to the saints of the most High; and the time came that the saints possessed the kingdom."
Daniel 7:22 KJV

"I saw in the night visions, and behold, one like the Son of man came with the clouds of heaven, and came to the Ancient of days, and they brought him near before him."

Daniel 7:13 KJV

"until the Ancient of days came, and judgment was given to the saints of the most High; and the time came that the saints possessed the kingdom."
Daniel 7:22 KJV

"And there was war in heaven: Michael and his angels fought against the dragon; and the dragon fought and his angels and prevailed not; neither was their place found any more in heaven."
Revelation 12:7-8 KJV

"And there was war in heaven: Michael and his angels fought against the dragon; and the dragon fought and his angels and prevailed not; neither was their place found any more in heaven."
Revelation 12:7-8 KJV

Now I would like to say, that the second heaven is the second planet from the sun, perhaps. Perhaps the answer is there is a hell on the second planet as to why they are in darkness. I believe I have found signs where they are held in a place back in time. So eighter these angels are from a earlier period in heaven. Are they were cast back in time before the sun existed and the stars. So, Enoch 21 explains, he is taken back to a period before the universe appears to be made.

So, to me it's as if this is a former creation or early creation. Many might think would make the earth older than the stars. Well perhaps, but perhaps Christ jumped back in time to a period before the worlds or seven stars were created to create Heaven. Whether this be chains under darkness or cast into outer darkness, it may be being cast back in time before things are fully created.

"And the angels which kept not their first estate, but left their own habitation, he hath reserved in everlasting chains under darkness unto the judgment of the great day."
Jude 1:6 KJV

"Then said the king to the servants, bind him hand and foot, and take him away, and cast him into outer darkness; there shall be weeping and gnashing of teeth."
Matthew 22:13 KJV

Enoch 21

2 And there I beheld neither the tremendous workmanship of an exalted heaven, nor of an established earth, but a desolate spot, prepared, and terrific.

3 There, too, I beheld seven stars of heaven bound in it together, like great mountains, and like a blazing fire. I exclaimed, for what species of crime have they been bound, and why have they been removed to this place? Then Uriel, one of the holy angels who was with me, and who conducted me, answered: Enoch, wherefore dost thou ask; wherefore reason with thyself, and anxiously inquire? These are those of the stars which have transgressed the commandment of the most high God; and are here bound, until the infinite number of the days of their crimes be completed.

So, these Grigori appear to be from an earlier period, or this is them jumping back in time to that place. Or being cast back in time before those things are created.

Secrets of Enoch 18

3 And they said to me: These are the Grigori, who with their prince Satanail rejected the Lord of light, and after them are those who are held in great darkness on the second heaven, and three of them went down on to earth from the Lord's throne, to the place Armon, and broke through their vows on the shoulder of the hill Armon and saw the daughters of men how good they are, and took to themselves wives, and befouled the earth with their deeds, who in all times of their age made lawlessness and mixing, and giants are born and marvelous big men and great enmity.

It's my belief after Christ ascended the throne at the second coming, these angels turned on God. Some of the following accounts speak somewhat for themselves.

So, what the Secrets of Enoch suggest, is three fallen angels, go back in time from the throne of God. Or these three from his very throne turned and went back in time to where Satan was, or the first star which fell.

Enoch 89

29 And I saw a throne erected in a delectable land.

30 Upon this sat the Lord of the sheep, who received all the sealed books.

31 Which were open before him.

32 Then the Lord called the first seven white ones, and commanded them to bring before him the first of the first stars,

Secrets of Enoch 18

3 And they said to me: These are the Grigori, who with their prince Satanail rejected the Lord of light, and after them are those who are held in great darkness on the second heaven, and three of them went down on to earth from the Lord's throne, to the place Ermon, and broke through their vows on the shoulder of the hill Ermon and saw the daughters of men how good they are, and took to themselves wives, and befouled the earth with their deeds, who in all times of their age made lawlessness and mixing, and giants are born and marvelous big men and great enmity.

Just things to study, seeing there are aliens here according to the books, and for a while Satan Had access to time travel. So, it appears as if sometimes during the resurrection a war broke out by those against God or Christ here, I am thinking. They had hoped to, breed men out, mix and cause man to become extinct. All this, and time travel, that its possible Satan though destroyed let say 7500 years ago. That if he jumped back and forth in time to many periods of time. He would still appear in many places long after he was imprisoned or bound. Because he would still appear in those places he visited in time, long after he is gone.

"And he laid hold on the dragon, that old serpent, which is the Devil, and Satan, and bound him a thousand years,"
Revelation 20:2 KJV

"And when the thousand years are expired, Satan shall be loosed out of his prison,"
Revelation 20:7 KJV

"and cast him into the bottomless pit, and shut him up, and set a seal upon him, that he should deceive the nations no more, till the thousand years should be fulfilled: and after that he must be loosed a little season."

Revelation 20:3 KJV

"And when they shall have finished their testimony, the beast that ascendeth out of the bottomless pit shall make war against them, and shall overcome them, and kill them."

Revelation 11:7 KJV

"and cast him into the bottomless pit, and shut him up, and set a seal upon him, that he should deceive the nations no more, till the thousand years should be fulfilled: and after that he must be loosed a little season."

Revelation 20:3 KJV

"And the fifth angel sounded, and I saw a star fall from heaven unto the earth: and to him was given the key of the bottomless pit."

Revelation 9:1 KJV

"And I saw an angel come down from heaven, having the key of the bottomless pit and a great chain in his hand."

Revelation 20:1 KJV

"And he opened the bottomless pit; and there arose a smoke out of the pit, as the smoke of a great furnace; and the sun and the air were darkened by reason of the smoke of the pit."

Revelation 9:2 KJV

THE TEACHING OF MICHAEL

Prophecy of God

"And I beheld when he had opened the sixth seal, and, lo, there was a great earthquake; and the sun became black as sackcloth of hair, and the moon became as blood; and the stars of heaven fell unto the earth, even as a fig tree casteth her untimely figs, when she is shaken of a mighty wind.

And the heaven departed as a scroll when it is rolled together; and every mountain and island were moved out of their places.

And the kings of the earth, and the great men, and the rich men, and the chief captains, and the mighty men, and every bondman, and every free man, hid themselves in the dens and in the rocks of the mountains; and said to the mountains and rocks, Fall on us, and hide us from the face of him that sitteth on the throne, and from the wrath of the Lamb: For the great day of his wrath is come; and who shall be able to stand?"
Revelation 6:12-17 KJV
Enoch 89
26 I saw also that the Lord of the sheep came to them, and taking in his hand the sceptre of his wrath seized the earth, which became rent asunder; while all the beasts and birds of heaven fell from the sheep, and sunk into the earth, which closed over them.

That because the resurrection men won't be able to die, among other effects in the weather and with the nature of natural things in life and human life. All will be effected due to the fact time is stuck together. The question remains of is Christ the ancient of days already raised? And is there another still in the earth, are not yet come?

"And in those days shall men seek death, and shall not find it; and shall desire to die, and death shall flee from them."
Revelation 9:6 KJV

Letters of Herod and Pilot
Now when he was crucified, there was darkness over all the world, and the sun was obscured for half a day, and the stars appeared, but no lustre was seen in them; and the moon lost its brightness, as though tinged with blood; and the world of the departed was swallowed up; so that the very sanctuary of the temple, as they call it, did not appear to the Jews themselves at their fall, but they perceived a chasm in the earth, and the rolling of successive thunders. And amid this terror the dead appeared rising again, as the Jews themselves bore witness,

So, like the ship I saw move along the Hayward fault, all these things are effected and open due to seven times the pressure on the earth. And the dead are raised and many other can't die. These are the elect, and those saved from the earth when seized at the outset.

"Blessed and holy is he that hath part in the first resurrection: on such the second death hath no power, but they shall be priests of God and of Christ, and shall reign with him a thousand years."
Revelation 20:6 KJV

BUT WHAT WE DON'T SEE IS THIS MONEYLESS SYSTEM BEING TAUGHT THROUGHOUT THE BIBLE

"And when he had opened the third seal, I heard the third beast say, Come and see. And I beheld, and lo a black horse; and he that sat on him had a pair of balances in his hand. And I heard a voice in the midst of the four beasts say, A measure of wheat for a penny, and three measures of barley for a penny; and see thou hurt not the oil and the wine."
Revelation 6:5-6 KJV

So, my study involved uncovering how a moneyless system should work. It's actually a balance between, available and produced goods, using your own system, of dividing all produced. Between all the inhabitants of the land. To farmers farm land divisions, all work divided, all goods divided stored or saved, for the purpose of equal division. So actually this is the Archangel doctrine which I ascribe to.

"And all that believed were together and had all things common; and sold their possessions and goods, and parted them to all men, as every man had need. And they, continuing daily with one accord in the temple, and breaking bread from house to house, did eat their meat with gladness and singleness of heart, praising God, and having favor with all the people. And the Lord added to the church daily such as should be saved."
Acts 2:44-47 KJV

"Fulfil ye my joy, that ye be likeminded, having the same love, being of one accord, of one mind. Let nothing be done through strife or vainglory; but in lowliness of mind let each esteem other better than themselves. Look not every man on his own things, but every man also on the things of others. Let this mind be in you, which was also in Christ Jesus:"
Philippians 2:2-5 KJV

"And when the children of Israel saw it, they said one to another, It is manna: for they wist not what it was. And Moses said unto them, this is the bread which the LORD hath given you to eat. This is the thing which the LORD hath commanded, gather of it every man according to his eating, an omer for every man, according to the number of your persons; take ye every man for them which are in his tents. And the children of Israel did so, and gathered, some more, some less. And when they did mete it with an omer, he that gathered much had nothing over, and he that gathered little had no lack; they gathered every man according to his eating."
Exodus 16:15-18 KJV

What is an omer equal to?
In traditional Jewish standards of measurement, the omer was equivalent to the volume of 43.2 chicken's eggs, or what is also known as one-tenth of an ephah (three seahs). In dry weight, the omer weighed between 1.56–1.77 kg (3.4–3.9 lb), being the quantity of flour required to separate therefrom the dough offering.

"But in those days, after that tribulation, the sun shall be darkened, and the moon shall not give her light, and the stars of heaven shall fall, and the powers that are in heaven shall be shaken. And then shall they see the son of man coming in the clouds with great power and glory. And then shall he send his angels and shall gather together his elect from the four winds, from the uttermost part of the earth to the uttermost part of heaven."
Mark 13:24-27 KJV

"Then Jesus said unto them, Verily, verily, I say unto you, Moses gave you not that bread from heaven; but my Father giveth you the true bread from heaven. For the bread of God is he which cometh down from heaven, and giveth life unto the world."

John 6:32-33 KJV

THOSE SENT TO TEACH IN THE 1000 YEAR PERIOD

"Blessed and holy is he that hath part in the first resurrection: on such the second death hath no power, but they shall be priests of God and of Christ, and shall reign with him a thousand years."
Revelation 20:6 KJV

Undoubtedly the place Enoch is taken is some point in the future or after those of the future came back in time.
Enoch 17
1 They raised me up into a certain place, where there was the appearance of a burning fire; and when they pleased they assumed the likeness of men.

"And of the angels he saith, Who maketh his angels spirits, And his ministers a flame of fire."
Hebrews 1:7 KJV

"And the angel of the LORD appeared unto him in a flame of fire out of the midst of a bush: and he looked, and, behold, the bush burned with fire, and the bush was not consumed."
Exodus 3:2 KJV

"And when forty years were expired, there appeared to him in the wilderness of mount Sina an angel of the Lord in a flame of fire in a bush."
Acts 7:30 KJV

"For it came to pass, when the flame went up toward heaven from off the altar, that the angel of the LORD ascended in the flame of the altar. And Manoah and his wife looked on it, and fell on their faces to the ground. But the angel of the LORD did no more appear to Manoah and to his wife. Then Manoah knew that he was an angel of the LORD."
Judges 13:20-21 KJV

Now notice, the Angel that appears to Manoah and his wife says his name is a secret. Because these Angels in most cases are from the resurrection at the end. Further there may be some angels who have not yet been born, much less resurrected. But do to time travel we are seeing them giving us evidence this teaching is true.

"And the angel of the LORD said unto him, why askest thou thus after my name, seeing it is secret?"
Judges 13:18 KJV

Yet when Christ talking about a thing which hasn't yet happened tells them it happened. Why, because they are all come from the resurrection and have broken the Time Barrier.

"And Jesus answered and said unto them, Elias truly shall first come, and restore all things. But I say unto you, That Elias is come already, and they knew him not, but have done unto him whatsoever they listed. Likewise, shall also the Son of man suffer of them."
Matthew 17:11-12 KJV

Tobit 12
14 And now God hath sent me to heal thee and Sara thy daughter in law.
15 I am Raphael, one of the seven holy angels, which present the prayers of the saints, and which go in and out before the glory of the Holy One.

But yet, much like Manoah and his wife Time Travel is being kept a secret. All these are those of the first resurrection being made ministers and flames of fire. Those sent out from the end to teach us before the end.

"And as they came down from the mountain, he charged them that they should tell no man what things they had seen, till the Son of man were risen from the dead."
Mark 9:9 KJV

Bottomless Pit

Enoch 89

29 And I saw a throne erected in a delectable land;

30 Upon this sat the Lord of the sheep, who received all the sealed books;

31 Which were open before him.

32 Then the Lord called the first seven white ones and commanded them to bring before him the first of the first stars,

Now after this, the world is become the world of the angels. And in these days the angels are judged. And Satan shall be loosed and shall deceive the angels of God, and had he continued no Angel would remain. But he shall be cast into the bottomless pit. Not into the earth, to stop the Time Loop of happing with evil still in the earth.

"And I saw an angel come down from heaven, having the key of the bottomless pit and a great chain in his hand. And he laid hold on the dragon, that old serpent, which is the Devil, and Satan, and bound him a thousand years, and cast him into the bottomless pit, and shut him up, and set a seal upon him, that he should deceive the nations no more, till the thousand years should be fulfilled: and after that he must be loosed a little season."
Revelation 20:1-3 KJV

"And when the thousand years are expired, Satan shall be loosed out of his prison, and shall go out to deceive the nations which are in the four quarters of the earth, Gog and Magog, to gather them together to battle: the number of whom is as the sand of the sea."
Revelation 20:7-8 KJV

"But the rest of the dead lived not again until the thousand years were finished. This is the first resurrection."
Revelation 20:5 KJV

"And I stood upon the sand of the sea, and saw a beast rise up out of the sea, having seven heads and ten horns, and upon his horns ten crowns, and upon his heads the name of blasphemy."
Revelation 13:1 KJV

"And I will give power unto my two witnesses, and they shall prophesy a thousand two hundred and threescore days, clothed in sackcloth. These are the two olive trees, and the two candlesticks standing before the God of the earth. And if any man will hurt them, fire proceedeth out of their mouth, and devoureth their enemies: and if any man will hurt them, he must in this manner be killed. These have power to shut heaven, that it rain not in the days of their prophecy: and have power over waters to turn them to blood, and to smite the earth with all plagues, as often as they will. And when they shall have finished their testimony, the beast that ascendeth out of the bottomless pit shall make war against them, and shall overcome them, and kill them."
Revelation 11:3-7 KJV

THESE ARE THOSE WHO REESTABLISH THE MONETARY SYSTEM

"And I beheld another beast coming up out of the earth; and he had two horns like a lamb, and he spake as a dragon. And he exerciseth all the power of the first beast before him, and causeth the earth and them which dwell therein to worship the first beast, whose deadly wound was healed. And he doeth great wonders, so that he maketh fire come down from heaven on the earth in the sight of men,"
Revelation 13:11-13 KJV

"And the fifth angel sounded, and I saw a star fall from heaven unto the earth: and to him was given the key of the bottomless pit."
Revelation 9:1 KJV

"And when the thousand years are expired, Satan shall be loosed out of his prison, and shall go out to deceive the nations which are in the four quarters of the earth, Gog and Magog, to gather them together to battle: the number of whom is as the sand of the sea.
Revelation 20:7 KJV

"And he causeth all, both small and great, rich and poor, free and bond, to receive a mark in their right hand, or in their foreheads:"
Revelation 13:16 KJV

"And it shall be, as with the people, so with the priest; as with the servant, so with his master; as with the maid, so with her mistress; as with the buyer, so with the seller; as with the lender, so with the borrower; as with the taker of usury, so with the giver of usury to him. The land shall be utterly emptied, and utterly spoiled: for the LORD hath spoken this word. Therefore hath the curse devoured the earth, and they that dwell therein are desolate: therefore the inhabitants of the earth are burned, and few men left."

Isaiah 24:2-3, 6 KJV

Esdras 12:23

23 In his last days shall the most High raise up three kingdoms, and renew many things therein, and they shall have the dominion of the earth,

Esdras 12:

24 For these are they that shall accomplish his wickedness, and that shall finish his last

Esdras 13

25 This is the meaning of the vision: Whereas thou sawest a man coming up from the midst of the sea:

26 The same is he whom God the Highest hath kept a great season, which by his own self shall deliver his creature: and he shall order them that are left behind.

27 And whereas thou sawest, that out of his mouth there came as a blast of wind, and fire, and storm;

28 And that he held neither sword, nor any instrument of war, but that the rushing in of him destroyed the whole multitude that came to subdue him; this is the interpretation:

"I beheld, and the same horn made war with the saints, and prevailed against them; until the Ancient of days came, and judgment was given to the saints of the most High; and the time came that the saints possessed the kingdom."

Daniel 7:21-22 KJV

"Then I heard one saint speaking, and another saint said unto that certain saint which spake, How long shall be the vision concerning the daily sacrifice, and the transgression of desolation, to give

both the sanctuary and the host to be trodden under foot? And he said unto me, unto two thousand and three hundred days; then shall the sanctuary be cleansed."
Daniel 8:13-14 KJV

Esdras 13

5 And after this I beheld, and, lo, there was gathered together a multitude of men, out of number, from the four winds of the heaven, to subdue the man that came out of the sea

6 But I beheld, and, lo, he had graved himself a great mountain, and flew up upon

7 And after this I beheld, and, lo, all they which were gathered together to subdue him were sore afraid, and yet durst fight.

8 And, lo, as he saw the violence of the multitude that came, he neither lifted up his hand, nor held sword, nor any instrument of war:

9 But only I saw that he sent out of his mouth as it had been a blast of fire, and out of his lips a flaming breath, and out of his tongue he cast out sparks and tempests.

10 And they were all mixed together; the blast of fire, the flaming breath, and the great tempest; and fell with violence upon the multitude which was prepared to fight, and burned them up everyone, so that upon a sudden of an innumerable multitude nothing was to be perceived, but only dust and smell of smoke: when I saw this I was afraid.

11 Afterward saw I the same man come down from the mountain, and call unto him another peaceable Multitude.

And they went up on the breadth of the earth, and compassed the camp of the saints about, and the beloved city: and fire came down from God out of heaven and devoured them. And the devil that deceived them was cast into the lake of fire and brimstone, where the beast and the false prophet are, and shall be tormented day and night for ever and ever.
Revelation 20:7-10 KJV

The point here is that I don't think the battle of Armageddon will happen until after the thousand year period has passed. That we are well into the prophecy. It won't happen until the evil people of the earth get resurrected after the thousand-year period has passed.

And when they are raised evil will spread over the earth. You see these are also angel from Heaven who turns against God. Also, the evil resurrected of the earth, who will begin to practice money making again.

Based on
"For where two or three are gathered together in my name, there am I in the midst of them."
Matthew 18:20 KJV

"And he said, Go thy way, Daniel: for the words are closed up and sealed till the time of the end."
Daniel 12:9 KJV

closed
/klōzd/
not open.

seal1
/sē(ə)l/
past tense: sealed; past participle: sealed
1. fasten or close securely.

"But thou, O Daniel, shut up the words, and seal the book, even to the time of the end: many shall run to and fro, and knowledge shall be increased."
Daniel 12:4 KJV

THE TRUE TEACHING IS FOUNDED ON TWO OR THREE

"And he said unto them, Verily I say unto you, that there be some of them that stand here, which shall not taste of death, till they have seen the kingdom of God come with power."
Mark 9:1 KJV

"Verily I say unto you, there be some standing here, which shall not taste of death, till they see the Son of man coming in his kingdom."
Matthew 16:28 KJV

"But I tell you of a truth, there be some standing here, which shall not taste of death, till they see the kingdom of God."
Luke 9:27 KJV

"And when the seven thunders had uttered their voices, I was about to write: and I heard a voice from heaven saying unto me, seal up those things which the seven thunders uttered, and write them not."
Revelation 10:4 KJV

Well I assume, the seven thunders will speak seven times stronger, as with the wind and the storms and the lighting. And for a time, those things are held back for the dead to be raised up.

"Thus saith the LORD of hosts, Behold, evil shall go forth from nation to nation, and a great whirlwind shall be raised up from the coasts of the earth."
Jeremiah 25:32 KJV

2nd Esdras 5
1 Nevertheless as coming the tokens, behold, the days shall come, that they which dwell upon earth shall be taken in a great number, and the way of truth shall be hidden, and the land shall be barren of faith.
2 But iniquity shall be increased above that which now thou seest, or that thou hast heard long ago.
And the land, that thou seest now to have root, shalt thou see wasted suddenly.
3 But if the most High grant thee to live, thou shalt see after the third trumpet that the sun shall suddenly shine again in the night, and the moon thrice in the day:
4 And blood shall drop out of wood, and the stone shall give his voice, and the people shall be troubled:

So that these events written are the result of Time being stuck together. So, all the former things will end. So, I would not let a man tell me these things are done.

Or these things are happening, when God told you, you would not understand until the end. Believing all you imagine, and nothing written you are like blind men, imagining all things.

"And after these things I saw four angels standing on the four corners of the earth, holding the four winds of the earth, that the wind should not blow on the earth, nor on the sea, nor on any tree.

And I saw another angel ascending from the east, having the seal of the living God: and he cried with a loud voice to the four angels, to whom it was given to hurt the earth and the sea, saying, Hurt not the earth, neither the sea, nor the trees, till we have sealed the servants of our God in their foreheads."
Revelation 7:1-3 KJV

And again, the angel ascending out of the east is an Angel being resurrected from the earth. These are those Christ would send at his coming. These are those also who teach.

So Daniel is told they would not understand until the end. Even after seeing the Kingdom of God come with Time Stuck Together for seven millennium at the resurrection of Christ and those from all periods of time.

As Michael said In Nicodemus Charinus and Lenthius they could not declare the Mysteries of God. But yet, I Michael in the middle of the seventh week do understand these things. As also the prophecy of Enoch told you, we would.
Nicodemus 21

These are the divine and sacred mysteries which we saw and heard. I, Charinus and Lenthius are not allowed to declare the other mysteries of God, as the archangel Michael ordered us,

2 Saying, ye shall go with my brethren to Jerusalem, and shall continue in prayers, declaring and glorifying the resurrection of Jesus Christ, seeing he hath raised you from the dead at the same time with himself.

3 And ye shall not talk with any man but sit as dumb persons till the time come when the Lord will allow you to relate the mysteries of his divinity.

4 The archangel Michael farther commanded us to go beyond Jordan, to an excellent and fat country, where there are many who rose from the dead along with us for the proof of the resurrection of Christ.

And again other books written which tell you are all wrong. But believing yourselves more than the books you are become blind men. Lovers of yourself and not of God.

Levi 5

11 And in the seventh week shall become priests, who are idolaters, adulterers, lovers of money, proud, lawless, lascivious, abusers of children and beasts.

12 And after their punishment shall have come from the Lord, the priesthood shall fail.

13 Then shall the Lord raise up a new priest.

Enoch 92

12 Afterwards, in the seventh week, a perverse generation shall arise; abundant shall be its deeds, and all its deeds perverse. During its completion, the righteous shall be selected from the everlasting plant of righteousness; and to them shall be given the sevenfold doctrine of his whole creation.

This is the Time foretold you would understand the mysteries of God. And consider the seventh angel, but not understanding you will not know, these angels are first men. And that many have to overcome Satan as well as the Beast.

They are required to overcome the false teaching which is established based on lies and acts of men. Men who profess being of God yet reject the teachings of God. Which they themselves replace with lies and traditions making illusions of established doctrines. But all of which are changed from its true teaching.

Jasher 6

11 And on that day, the Lord caused the whole earth to shake, and the sun darkened, and the foundations of the world raged, and the whole earth was moved violently, and the lightning flashed, and the thunder roared, and all the fountains in the earth were broken up, such as was not known to the inhabitants before; and God did this mighty act, in order to terrify the sons of men, that there might be no more evil upon earth.

12 And still the sons of men would not return from their evil ways, and they increased the anger of the Lord at that time and did not even direct their hearts to all this.

13 And at the end of seven days, in the six hundredth year of the life of Noah, the waters of the flood were upon the earth.

14 And all the fountains of the deep were broken up, and the windows of heaven were opened, and the rain was upon the earth forty days and forty nights.

Enoch 88

2 Again I lifted up my eyes towards heaven and saw a lofty roof. Above it were seven cataracts, which poured forth on a certain village much water.

9 Again I looked in the vision until those cataracts from that lofty roof were removed, and the fountains of the earth became equalized, while other depths were opened.

10 Into which the water began to descend, until the dry ground appeared.

EPIGRAPH

Telepathy At a Distance

I was backing my truck up to a client's dock, as I was bumping the dock.

A thought popped into my head that my ex-wife after a few years of separation and divorce was talking with my mother. I did not note the time, because I doubted my mom would remember that specific. But when I got home some hours later, my mom said I talked to your ex-wife today. (Calling her by her name of course)

Point: I did not know what they talked about, but I know it's possible to know what they talked about. God saw fit, not to give me that ability so I accept that. But I know it's possible to know more. This is the same spirit recorded in the books of God, and no man can prove that wrong, by God standards.

CHAPTER 13
RESURRECTION

Prophecy of God
"And I beheld when he had opened the sixth seal, and, lo, there was a great earthquake; and the sun became black as sackcloth of hair, and the moon became as blood; and the stars of heaven fell unto the earth, even as a fig tree casteth her untimely figs, when she is shaken of a mighty wind. And the heaven departed as a scroll when it is rolled together; and every mountain and island were moved out of their places.

And the kings of the earth, and the great men, and the rich men, and the chief captains, and the mighty men, and every bondman, and every free man, hid themselves in the dens and in the rocks of the mountains; and said to the mountains and rocks, Fall on us, and hide us from the face of him that sitteth on the throne, and from the wrath of the Lamb: For the great day of his wrath is come; and who shall be able to stand?"
Revelation 6:12-17 KJV

Enoch 89
26 I saw also that the Lord of the sheep came to them, and taking in his hand the sceptre of his wrath seized the earth, which became rent asunder; while all the beasts and birds of heaven fell from the sheep, and sunk into the earth, which closed over them.

That because the resurrection men won't be able to die, among other effects in the weather and with the nature of natural things in life and human life. All will be effected due to the fact time is stuck together. The question remains of is Christ the ancient of days already raised? And is there another still in the earth, are not yet come?

"And in those days shall men seek death, and shall not find it; and shall desire to die, and death shall flee from them."

Revelation 9:6 KJV

Letters of Herod and Pilot
Now when he was crucified, there was darkness over all the world, and the sun was obscured for half a day, and the stars appeared, but no lustre was seen in them; and the moon lost its brightness, as though tinged with blood; and the world of the departed was swallowed up; so that the very sanctuary of the temple, as they call it, did not appear to the Jews themselves at their fall, but they perceived a chasm in the earth, and the rolling of successive thunders. And amid this terror the dead appeared rising again, as the Jews themselves bore witness,

So, like the ship we saw one which moved along the Hayward fault, all these things are effected and open due to seven times the pressure on the earth. And the dead are raised and many other can't die. These are the elect, and those saved from the earth when seized at the outset.

"Blessed and holy is he that hath part in the first resurrection: on such the second death hath no power, but they shall be priests of God and of Christ, and shall reign with him a thousand years."
Revelation 20:6 KJV

MONEYLESS SYSTEM IS ESTABLISHED

"And when he had opened the third seal, I heard the third beast say, Come and see. And I beheld, and lo a black horse; and he that sat on him had a pair of balances in his hand. And I heard a voice in the midst of the four beasts say, A measure of wheat for a penny, and three measures of barley for a penny; and see thou hurt not the oil and the wine."
Revelation 6:5-6 KJV

"And he laid hold on the dragon, that old serpent, which is the Devil, and Satan, and bound him a thousand years,"
Revelation 20:2 KJV

"But in those days, after that tribulation, the sun shall be darkened, and the moon shall not give her light, and the stars of heaven shall fall, and the powers that are in heaven shall be shaken. And then shall they see the Son of man coming in the clouds with great power and glory. And then shall he send his angels, and shall gather together his elect from the four winds, from the uttermost part of the earth to the uttermost part of heaven."
Mark 13:24-27 KJV

BOTTOMLESS PIT

Enoch 89
29 And I saw a throne erected in a delectable land;
30 Upon this sat the Lord of the sheep, who received all the sealed books;
31 Which were open before him.
32 Then the Lord called the first seven white ones and commanded them to bring before him the first of the first stars,

Now after this, the world is become the world of the angels. And in these days the angels are judged. And Satan shall be loosed and shall deceive the angels of God, and had he continued no Angel would remain. But he shall be cast into the bottomless pit. Not into the earth, to stop the Time Loop of happing with evil still in the earth. Because by the fallen angels jumping back in time did they do it in a way

"And I saw an angel come down from heaven, having the key of the bottomless pit and a great chain in his hand. And he laid hold on the dragon, that old serpent, which is the Devil, and Satan, and bound him a thousand years, and cast him into the bottomless pit, and shut him up, and set a seal upon him, that he should deceive the nations no more, till the thousand years should be fulfilled: and after that he must be loosed a little season."
Revelation 20:1-3 KJV

"And when the thousand years are expired, Satan shall be loosed out of his prison, and shall go out to deceive the nations which are in the four quarters of the earth, Gog and Magog, to gather them together to battle: the number of whom is as the sand of the sea."
Revelation 20:7-8 KJV

"But the rest of the dead lived not again until the thousand years were finished. This is the first resurrection."
Revelation 20:5 KJV

"And I stood upon the sand of the sea, and saw a beast rise up out of the sea, having seven heads and ten horns, and upon his horns ten crowns, and upon his heads the name of blasphemy."
Revelation 13:1 KJV

"And I will give power unto my two witnesses, and they shall prophesy a thousand two hundred and threescore days, clothed in sackcloth. These are the two olive trees, and the two candlesticks standing before the God of the earth. And if any man will hurt them, fire proceedeth out of their mouth, and devoureth their enemies: and if any man will hurt them, he must in this manner be killed. These have power to shut heaven, that it rain not in the days of their prophecy: and have power over waters to turn them to blood, and to smite the earth with all plagues, as often as they will. And when they shall have finished their testimony, the beast that ascendeth out of the bottomless pit shall make war against them, and shall overcome them, and kill them."
Revelation 11:3-7 KJV

Nicodemus 20
2 And two very ancient men met them, and were asked by the saints, Who are ye, who have not yet been with us in hell, and have had your bodies placed in Paradise?
3 One of them answering, said, I am Enoch, who was translated by the word of God: [note: Gen. v. 24.] and this man who is with me, is Elijah the Tishbite, who was translated in a fiery chariot.
4 Here we have hitherto been, and have not tasted death, but are now about to return at the coming of Antichrist, being armed with divine signs and miracles, to engage with him in battle, and to be

slain by him at Jerusalem, and to be taken up alive again into the clouds, after three days and a half.

THESE ARE THOSE WHO REESTABLISH THE MONETARY SYSTEM

After the resurrection something comes up after the thousand year period has passed. So, perhaps some aliens get resurrected or released from being held for some time, in another point in time in our past even millions of years.

"And I beheld another beast coming up out of the earth; and he had two horns like a lamb, and he spake as a dragon. And he exerciseth all the power of the first beast before him, and causeth the earth and them which dwell therein to worship the first beast, whose deadly wound was healed. And he doeth great wonders, so that he maketh fire come down from heaven on the earth in the sight of men,"
Revelation 13:11-13 KJV

"And the fifth angel sounded, and I saw a star fall from heaven unto the earth: and to him was given the key of the bottomless pit."
Revelation 9:1 KJV

"And when the thousand years are expired, Satan shall be loosed out of his prison, and shall go out to deceive the nations which are in the four quarters of the earth, Gog and Magog, to gather them together to battle: the number of whom is as the sand of the sea.
Revelation 20:7 KJV

"And he causeth all, both small and great, rich and poor, free and bond, to receive a mark in their right hand, or in their foreheads:"
Revelation 13:16 KJV

"And it shall be, as with the people, so with the priest; as with the servant, so with his master; as with the maid, so with her mistress; as with the buyer, so with the seller; as with the lender, so with the borrower; as with the taker of usury, so with the giver of usury to him. The land shall be utterly emptied, and utterly spoiled: for the LORD hath spoken this word. Therefore hath the curse devoured the earth, and they that dwell therein are desolate: therefore the inhabitants of the earth are burned, and few men left."
Isaiah 24:2-3, 6 KJV

These three kingdoms I believe are raised up during the thousand years of peace. So, after the resurrection and reconstruction these kingdom will rise. So, this period during the resurrection many books speak on in our future. So, that the battle of the apocalypse really wont happen until the one called Satan is released, he who kills the two witnesses, makes fire come down from heaven and deceived the who earth after they are like angels and resurrected.

Esdras 12:23
23 In his last days shall the most High raise up three kingdoms, and renew many things therein, and they shall have the dominion of the earth,

Esdras 12:
25 For these are they that shall accomplish his wickedness, and that shall finish his last

Esdras 13
25 This is the meaning of the vision: Whereas thou sawest a man coming up from the midst of the sea:

26 The same is he whom God the Highest hath kept a great season, which by his own self shall deliver his creature: and he shall order them that are left behind.

27 And whereas thou sawest, that out of his mouth there came as a blast of wind, and fire, and storm;

28 And that he held neither sword, nor any instrument of war, but that the rushing in of him destroyed the whole multitude that came to subdue him; this is the interpretation:

"I beheld, and the same horn made war with the saints, and prevailed against them; until the Ancient of days came, and judgment was given to the saints of the most High; and the time came that the saints possessed the kingdom."

"And at that time shall Michael stand up, the great prince which standeth for the children of thy people: and there shall be a time of trouble, such as never was since there was a nation even to that same time: and at that time thy people shall be delivered, every one that shall be found written in the book. And many of them that sleep in the dust of the earth shall awake, some to everlasting life, and some to shame and everlasting contempt. And they that be wise shall shine as the brightness of the firmament; and they that turn many to righteousness as the stars for ever and ever."
Daniel 12:1-3 KJV

"I have raised up one from the north, and he shall come: from the rising of the sun shall he call upon my name: and he shall come upon princes as upon mortar, and as the potter treadeth clay. Who hath declared from the beginning, that we may know? and before time, that we may say, He is righteous? yea, there is none that sheweth, yea, there is none that declareth, yea, there is none that heareth your words. The first shall say to Zion, Behold, behold them: and I will give to Jerusalem one that bringeth good tidings. For I beheld, and there was no man; even among them, and there was no counsellor, that, when I asked of them, could answer a word. Behold, they are all vanity; their works are nothing: their molten images are wind and confusion."
Isaiah 41:25-29 KJV

And out of one of them came forth a little horn, which waxed exceeding great, toward the south, and toward the east, and toward the pleasant land. And it waxed great, even to the host of heaven;

and it cast down some of the host and of the stars to the ground and stamped upon them. Yea, he magnified himself even to the prince of the host, and by him the daily sacrifice was taken away, and the place of his sanctuary was cast down. And an host was given him against the daily sacrifice by reason of transgression, and it cast down the truth to the ground; and it practiced, and prospered.
Daniel 7:21-22 KJV

Then I heard one saint speaking, and another saint said unto that certain saint which spake, How long shall be the vision concerning the daily sacrifice, and the transgression of desolation, to give both the sanctuary and the host to be trodden under foot? And he said unto me, unto two thousand and three hundred days; then shall the sanctuary be cleansed.
Daniel 8:13-14 KJV

Esdras 13

5 And after this I beheld, and, lo, there was gathered together a multitude of men, out of number, from the four winds of the heaven, to subdue the man that came out of the sea

6 But I beheld, and, lo, he had graved himself a great mountain, and flew up upon

7 And after this I beheld, and, lo, all they which were gathered together to subdue him were sore afraid, and yet durst fight.

8 And, lo, as he saw the violence of the multitude that came, he neither lifted up his hand, nor held sword, nor any instrument of war:

9 But only I saw that he sent out of his mouth as it had been a blast of fire, and out of his lips a flaming breath, and out of his tongue he cast out sparks and tempests.

10 And they were all mixed together; the blast of fire, the flaming breath, and the great tempest; and fell with violence upon the multitude which was prepared to fight, and burned them up everyone, so that upon a sudden of an innumerable multitude nothing was to be perceived, but only dust and smell of smoke: when I saw this I was afraid.

11 Afterward saw I the same man come down from the mountain and call unto him another peaceable Multitude.

"And they went up on the breadth of the earth, and compassed the camp of the saints about, and the beloved city: and fire came down from God out of heaven and devoured them. And the devil

that deceived them was cast into the lake of fire and brimstone, where the beast and the false prophet are, and shall be tormented day and night for ever and ever."
Revelation 20:7-10 KJV

The point here is that I don't think the battle of Armageddon will happen until after the thousand-year period has passed. That we are well into the prophecy. It won't happen until the evil people of the earth get resurrected after the thousand-year period has passed.

And when they are raised evil will spread over the earth. You see these are also angel from Heaven who turns against God. Also, the evil resurrected of the earth, who will begin to practice money making again.

Based on
"For where two or three are gathered together in my name, there am I in the midst of them."
Matthew 18:20 KJV

"And he said, Go thy way, Daniel: for the words are closed up and sealed till the time of the end."
Daniel 12:9 KJV

closed
/klōzd/
not open.

seal1
/sē(ə)l/
past tense: sealed; past participle: sealed
1.fasten or close securely.

"But thou, O Daniel, shut up the words, and seal the book, even to the time of the end: many shall run to and fro, and knowledge shall be increased."
Daniel 12:4 KJV

THE TRUE TEACHING IS FOUNDED ON 2 or 3

"And he said unto them, Verily I say unto you, that there be some of them that stand here, which shall not taste of death, till they have seen the kingdom of God come with power."
Mark 9:1 KJV

"Verily I say unto you, there be some standing here, which shall not taste of death, till they see the Son of man coming in his kingdom."
Matthew 16:28 KJV

"But I tell you of a truth, there be some standing here, which shall not taste of death, till they see the kingdom of God."
Luke 9:27 KJV

"And when the seven thunders had uttered their voices, I was about to write: and I heard a voice from heaven saying unto me, seal up those things which the seven thunders uttered, and write them not."
Revelation 10:4 KJV

Well, I assume, the seven thunders will speak seven times stronger, as with the wind and the storms and the lighting. And for a time, those things are held back for the dead to be raised up.

"Thus, saith the LORD of hosts, Behold, evil shall go forth from nation to nation, and a great whirlwind shall be raised up from the coasts of the earth."
Jeremiah 25:32 KJV

2nd Esdras 5

1 Nevertheless as coming the tokens, behold, the days shall come, that they which dwell upon earth shall be taken in a great number, and the way of truth shall be hidden, and the land shall be barren of faith.

2 But iniquity shall be increased above that which now thou seest, or that thou hast heard long ago. And the land, that thou seest now to have root, shalt thou see wasted suddenly.

3 But if the Most High grant thee to live, thou shalt see after the third trumpet that the sun shall suddenly shine again in the night, and the moon thrice in the day:

4 And blood shall drop out of wood, and the stone shall give his voice, and the people shall be troubled:

So that these events written are the result of Time being stuck together. So, all the former things will end. So, I would not let a man tell me these things are done.

Or these things are happening, when God told you, you would not understand until the end. Believing all you imagine, and nothing written you are like blind men, imagining all things.

"And after these things I saw four angels standing on the four corners of the earth, holding the four winds of the earth, that the wind should not blow on the earth, nor on the sea, nor on any tree.

And I saw another angel ascending from the east, having the seal of the living God: and he cried with a loud voice to the four angels, to whom it was given to hurt the earth and the sea, saying, Hurt not the earth, neither the sea, nor the trees, till we have sealed the servants of our God in their foreheads."
Revelation 7:1-3 KJV

And again the angel ascending out of the east is an Angel being resurrected from the earth. These are those Christ would send at his coming. These are those also who teach.

So, Daniel is told they would not understand until the end. Even after seeing the Kingdom of God come with Time Stuck Together for seven millennium at the resurrection of Christ and those from all periods of time.

As Michael said In Nicodemus Charinus and Lenthius they could not declare the Mysteries of God. But yet, I Michael in the middle of the seventh week do understand these things. As also the prophecy of Enoch told you, we would.

Nicodemus 21

These are the divine and sacred mysteries which we saw and heard. I, Charinus and Lenthius are not allowed to declare the other mysteries of God, as the archangel Michael ordered us,

2 Saying, ye shall go with my brethren to Jerusalem, and shall continue in prayers, declaring and glorifying the resurrection of Jesus Christ, seeing he hath raised you from the dead at the same time with himself.

3 And ye shall not talk with any man but sit as dumb persons till the time come when the Lord will allow you to relate the mysteries of his divinity.

4 The archangel Michael farther commanded us to go beyond Jordan, to an excellent and fat country, where there are many who rose from the dead along with us for the proof of the resurrection of Christ.

And again other books written which tell you are all wrong. But believing yourselves more than the books you are become blind men. Lovers of yourself and not of God.

Levi 5

11 And in the seventh week shall become priests, who are idolaters, adulterers, lovers of money, proud, lawless, lascivious, abusers of children and beasts.

12 And after their punishment shall have come from the Lord, the priesthood shall fail.

13 Then shall the Lord raise up a new priest.

Enoch 92

12 Afterwards, in the seventh week, a perverse generation shall arise; abundant shall be its deeds, and all its deeds perverse. During its completion, the righteous shall be selected from the everlasting plant of righteousness; and to them shall be given the sevenfold doctrine of his whole

creation.

This is the Time foretold you would understand the mysteries of God. And consider the seventh angel, but not understanding you will not know, these angels are first men. And that many have to overcome Satan as well as the Beast.

They are required to overcome the false teaching which is established based on lies and acts of men. Men who profess being of God yet reject the teachings of God. Which they themselves replace with lies and traditions making illusions of established doctrines. But all of which are changed from its true teaching.

But the Book of the Revelation tells you there is no longer Time. Why, because it has been stuck together to raise the dead, and to create all things. It opened the door for a man to be God. That without time all things are possible. From the invisible things to the visible things. That The Book of Revelation is written during this time when

"And I saw another mighty angel come down from heaven, clothed with a cloud: and a rainbow was upon his head, and his face was as it were the sun, and his feet as pillars of fire: and he had in his hand a little book open: and he set his right foot upon the sea, and his left foot on the earth, and cried with a loud voice, as when a lion roareth: and when he had cried, seven thunders uttered their voices. And when the seven thunders had uttered their voices, I was about to write: and I heard a voice from heaven saying unto me, Seal up those things which the seven thunders uttered, and write them not. And the angel which I saw stand upon the sea and upon the earth lifted up his hand to heaven, and sware by him that liveth for ever and ever, who created heaven, and the things that therein are, and the earth, and the things that therein are, and the sea, and the things which are therein, that there should be time no longer: but in the days of the voice of the seventh angel, when he shall begin to sound, the mystery of God should be finished, as he hath declared to his servants the prophets."
Revelation 10:1-7 KJV

So, when the church took these books and removed them and said they are not inspired of God. They themselves were not inspired by God. God was not their master in these things. Anytime you witness the dead rising and angels coming and going those very acts of God are an inspiration.

These men who reject, held to their own beliefs not of God, to hold down the word of God. With teachings in fact, which have little meaning, nor do they prove anything.

But leave me to wonder and make up what they will saying things about God not written in any book. But saying things they themselves have imagined. But all things should be done two or three.

By Prophets, Apostles and Witnesses that's the teaching. Not by things not written in any book proving God. Those things are of men and Satan

So when Christ told you "But I tell you of a truth, there be some standing here, which shall not taste of death, till they see the kingdom of God." he gave you evidence of the Kingdom of God and men hid it, and covered it up.

TIME STUCK TOGETHER

Letters of Herod and Pilot
Now when he was crucified, there was darkness over all the world, and the sun was obscured for half a day, and the stars appeared, but no lustre was seen in them; and the moon lost its brightness, as though tinged with blood; and the world of the departed was swallowed up; so that the very sanctuary of the temple, as they call it, did not appear to the Jews themselves at their fall, but they perceived a chasm in the earth, and the rolling of successive thunders.

And amid this terror the dead appeared rising again, as the Jews themselves bore witness, and said that it was Abraham, and Isaac, and Jacob, and the twelve patriarchs, and Moses, and Job, who had died before, as they say, some three thousand five hundred years.

And there were very many whom I myself saw appearing in the body, and they made lamentation over the Jews, because of the transgression, which was committed by them, and because of the destruction of the Jews and of their law.

And the terror of the earthquake continued from the sixth hour of the preparation until the ninth hour; and when it was evening on the first day of the week, there came a sound from heaven, and the heaven became seven times more luminous than on all other days. And at the third hour of the night the sun appeared more luminous than it had ever shone, lighting up the whole hemisphere.

And as lightning-flashes suddenly come forth in a storm, so there were seen men, lofty in stature, and surpassing in glory, a countless host, crying out, and their voice was heard as that of exceedingly loud thunder, Jesus that was crucified is risen again: come up from Hades ye that were enslaved in the subterraneous recesses of Hades.

And the chasm in the earth was as if it had no bottom; but it was so that the very foundations of the earth appeared, with those that shouted in heaven, and walked in the body among the dead that were raised. And He that raised up all the dead and bound Hades said, Say to my disciples He goeth before you into Galilee, there shall ye see Him. And all that night the light ceased not shining.

And many of the Jews died in the chasm of the earth, being swallowed up, so that on the morrow most of those who had been against Jesus were not to be found. Others saw the apparition of men rising again whom none of us had ever seen. One synagogue of the Jews was alone left in Jerusalem itself, for they all disappeared in that ruin.

Now when he was crucified darkness came over all the world; the sun was altogether hidden, and the sky appeared dark while it was yet day, so that the stars were seen, though still they had their lustre obscured, wherefore, I suppose your excellency is not unaware that in all the world they lighted their lamps from the sixth hour until evening. And the moon, which was like blood, did not shine all night long, although it was at the full, and the stars and Orion made lamentation over the Jews, because of the transgression committed by them. And on the first day of the week, about the third hour of the night, the sun appeared as it never shone before, and the whole heaven became bright. And as lightnings come in a storm, so certain men of lofty stature, in beautiful array, and of indescribable glory, appeared in the air, and a countless host of angels, crying out and saying, Glory to God in the highest, and on earth peace, good will among men: Come up from Hades, ye who are in bondage in the depths of Hades.

And at their voice all the mountains and hills were moved, and the rocks were rent, and great chasms were made in the earth, so that the very places of the abyss were visible.

And amid the terror dead men were seen rising again, so that the Jews who saw it said, We beheld Abraham and Isaac, and Jacob, and the twelve patriarchs, who died some two thousand five hundred years before, and we beheld Noah clearly in the body. And all the multitude walked about and sang hymns to God with a loud voice, saying, The Lord our God, who hath risen from the dead, hath made alive all the dead, and Hades he hath spoiled and slain.

Therefore, my lord king, all that night the light ceased not. But many of the Jews died, and were sunk and swallowed up in the chasms that night, so that not even their bodies were to be seen. Now I mean, that those of the Jews suffered who spake against Jesus. And but one synagogue remained in Jerusalem, for all the synagogues which had been against Jesus were overwhelmed.

Through that terror, therefore, being amazed and being seized with great trembling, in that very hour, I ordered what had been done by them all to be written, and I have sent it to thy mightiness. So, this is what will happen when Time is Stuck together to make no Time. The dead will be raised and we will be resurrected.

Well, I need no judgment of men, God will judge me. If I am wrong, he will punish me as a false prophet. But, I study his work, and by his teaching I teach. I seek redemption to God, if required I fall on my sword. Or, I pick up his cross and bear it. But I tell you, before you say I'm wrong look again at the books which say you are wrong, in God's name Amen.

PART 1

I heard a radio evangelist talk about the two angels sent when the burial stone at Christ tomb rolled away.

When you leave out the word men, you take away the point of the story, change its meaning altogether.

Why?

Men had not yet been resurrected, further they are resurrected in the 8th Day, that's about, what, 477 years by its number.

They stuck time together to raise the dead. The fact you saw it, has little to do with what you saw at the resurrection. More to do with them sticking time together to show you what was going to happen in the future. In which, the dead are actually raised, now during that time in the future, they reached back for us, from the future, taught and gave us the Books of God and the Bible "And while they looked stedfastly toward heaven as he went up, behold, two men stood by them in white apparel;"
Acts 1:10 KJV

Says, during the resurrection

The lost Gospel of Peter
9 And in the night in which the Lord's day was drawing on, as the soldiers kept guard two by two in a watch, there was a great voice in the heaven; and they saw the heavens opened, and two men descend from thence with great light and approach the tomb. And that stone which was put at the door rolled of itself and made way in part; and the tomb was opened, and both the young men entered in.

"And it came to pass, as they were much perplexed thereabout, behold, two men stood by them in shining garments:"
Luke 24:4 KJV

"And when he had opened the fifth seal, I saw under the altar the souls of them that were slain for the word of God, and for the testimony which they held:"
Revelation 6:9 KJV

At the time this is written they must wait, because time is in their way, and they can't live until time is removed. So, not all who are born have been born, we wait on them.

"And white robes were given unto every one of them; and it was said unto them, that they should rest yet for a little season, until their fellow servants also and their brethren, that should be killed as they were, should be fulfilled."
Revelation 6:11 KJV

Barnabas 13
So the other Fathers, begin the eighth day, that is, the beginning of the other world. 10 For which cause we observe the eighth day with gladness, in which Jesus rose from the dead; and having manifested himself to his disciples, ascended into heaven.

PART 2
"And entering into the sepulcher, they saw a young man sitting on the right side, clothed in a long white garment; and they were affrighted."
Mark 16:5 KJV

"He that overcometh, the same shall be clothed in white raiment; and I will not blot out his name out of the book of life, but I will confess his name before my Father, and before his angels."
Revelation 3:5 KJV
So, they tell us who we are, equal to angels, and these books record those who came back in time to assist others and give us the books, in which the men who rejected the books, rejected God. "neither can they die any more: for they are equal unto the angels; and are the children of God, being the children of the resurrection."

Luke 20:36 KJV

Secrets of Enoch 65

5 When all creation visible and invisible, as the Lord created it, shall end, then every man goes to the great judgement, and then all-time shall perish, and the years, and thenceforward there will be neither months nor days nor hours, they will be stuck together and will not be counted.

Note, this is the eighth day, which hasn't happened, yet has, because they reached back in time to us.

So, if we leave out the fact those angels are men, which shows you they had to come from the resurrection in the future, you altered the teaching.

"I saw under the altar the souls of them that were slain for the word of God, and for the testimony which they held:"
Revelation 6:9 KJV

Note: and this is because the latter generations are not yet born. And many of those are yet a

Now after this, the world is become the world of the angels. And in these days the angels are judged. And Satan shall be loosed and shall deceive the angels of God, and had he continued no Angel would remain. But he shall be cast into the bottomless pit. Not into the earth, to stop the Time Loop of happing with evil still in the earth.

"And I saw an angel come down from heaven, having the key of the bottomless pit and a great chain in his hand. And he laid hold on the dragon, that old serpent, which is the Devil, and Satan, and bound him a thousand years, and cast him into the bottomless pit, and shut him up, and set a seal upon him, that he should deceive the nations no more, till the thousand years should be fulfilled: and after that he must be loosed a little season."

PART 3

These are the "Seven Thunders" which must be held back, or they can destroy everything on the earth.

"And when the seven thunders had uttered their voices, I was about to write: and I heard a voice from heaven saying unto me, Seal up those things which the seven thunders uttered, and write them not."
Revelation 10:4 KJV

These angels are actually holding back parts of the atmosphere together, during the time the seven atmospheres get joined together.

Question? When time gets stuck together fires will burn more stronger unable to be put out. So, is the burning earth evidence time was stuck together, maybe so!

How long did the books say, it was to create all things. 7 days? 7,000 years? 13,000,000,000 years? This is in regards to the creation, which there is no correct number by our standards.
- Does this evidence prove time was sped up, due of the hostile conditions on earth at that time?

Enoch 68
26 By this oath the sea has been formed, and the foundation of it.
27 During the period of its fury he has established the sand against it, which continues unchanged for ever; and by this oath the abyss has been made strong; nor is it removable from its station for ever and ever.

Moses talking about time stuck together notes the change! Or the core being made during the period of fury.

"For a fire is kindled in mine anger, and shall burn unto the lowest hell, And shall consume the earth with her increase, And set on fire the foundations of the mountains."
Deuteronomy 32:22 KJV

So, the environment being described, for Time Stuck Together is. That the atmospheres from all seven millennium get compressed together to raise the dead, all whom they choose.

The earth were headed for, Is kind of like earth was when the Earth first formed? As if reverting back to something!

Science

At its beginning, Earth was unrecognizable from its modern form. At first, it was extremely hot, to the point that the planet likely consisted almost entirely of molten magma. Over the course of a few hundred million years, the planet began to cool, and oceans of liquid water formed.

What was the atmosphere like when the Earth was first formed?
When Earth formed 4.6 billion years ago from a hot mix of gases and solids, it had almost no atmosphere. The surface was molten. As Earth cooled, an atmosphere formed mainly from gases spewed from volcanoes. It included hydrogen sulfide, methane, and ten to 200 times as much carbon dioxide as today's atmosphere.

So, perhaps this burned because time being stuck together can cause this effect on the earth. So is it burning at creation because time is stuck together?

Many things I still formulate, trying to come to the right understanding requires you, bring most outlooks to the table to ascertain the most accurate view. Not corrupted by a group standard, so you are required to sell your soul to participate. Also holding yourselves to a very narrow viewpoint.

Renewal

This star is capable of time travel, I guess the importance of it is, how far back did it go. The Bottomless is created the first and second day. Seemingly the cores of planets.

Fact is on the fifth day; God made the stars. Unlike you all, I cannot see these as twenty-four-hour periods. I think though Time Travel is possible God fixed Time, but when in the creation did, he do it? That would matter in trying to understand creation and the length of time taken to create all things. Or was time altered then fixed?

Esdras 4:
37 By measure hath he measured the times; and by number hath he numbered the times; and he doth not move nor stir them, until the said measure be fulfilled.
So, Esdras 4:37 is saying Time is Consistent until a certain period. This period of Time Travel is also implying where God comes from. So, if Time Travel isn't started until our future, it points a finger at who and where God came from.

So, the fact would be Time is fixed until it's broken 13 or 14 billion years after creation. Though God jumped back or forward in Time, time would remain fixed until broken in about 480 years from now more or less. But this does not say, time was always fixed, it leaves a question about just what is fixed in time. Maybe just the time where stuck in is fixed? Looks like at least time may be calibrated for a particular period.

Enoch 81
8 Truly has been stated, and accurately has been computed that which is marked down; for the luminaries, the months, the fixed periods, the years, and the days, Uriel has explained to me, and communicated to me; whom the Lord of all creation, on my account, commanded (according to the might of heaven, and the power which it possesses both by night and by day) to explain the laws of light to man, of the sun, moon, and stars, and of all the powers of heaven, which are turned with their respective orbs.
9 This is the ordinance of the stars, which set in their places, in their seasons, in their periods, in their days, and in their months.

So, by these writings it appears Time is fixed which aids in our learning the creation and making science and calculations possible in all things. Which might also aid in the discovery of Time Travel by our learning.

set1

FELL BEFORE THEIR TIME ARRIVE = TIME TRAVEL

The crime of Time Travel, to fall before their time arrived. To go someplace before you were supposed to get there. And if you look at why the fallen angels are in big trouble they went back before their time arrived. Looking at that knowing time trouble exists, you might view this as some type time travel incursion into a place they didn't belong.

Enoch 18
14 And there I beheld seven stars, like great blazing mountains, and like spirits entreating me.
15 Then the angel said, this place, until the consummation of heaven and earth, will be the prison of the stars, and the host of heaven
16 The stars which roll over fire are those which transgressed the commandment of God before their time arrived; for they came not in their proper season. Therefore, was He offended with them, and bound them, until the period of the consummation of their crimes in the secret year.

Enoch 18
13 And in the columns of heaven I beheld fires, which descended without number, but neither on high, nor into the deep. Over these fountains also I perceived a place which had neither the firmament of heaven above it, nor the solid ground underneath it; neither was there water above it, nor anything on wing; but the spot was desolate.
14 And there I beheld seven stars, like great blazing mountains, and like spirits entreating me.
15 Then the angel said, this place, until the consummation of heaven and earth, will be the prison of the stars, and the host of heaven.

Chapter 21
1 Then I made a circuit to a place in which nothing was completed.
2 And there I beheld neither the tremendous workmanship of an exalted heaven, nor of an established earth, but a desolate spot, prepared, and terrific.

3 There, too, I beheld seven stars of heaven bound in it together, like great mountains, and like a blazing fire. I exclaimed, For what species of crime have they been bound, and why have they been removed to this place?

EPILOGUE

I recall one night as I slept, I saw a dark shadow the with the figure of a man standing in my room. Suddenly the dark figure came upon me. I screamed loudly waking up my mom, I would say about 1971. I kicked hard at the figure as I screamed out.

My mom ran into the room alarmed and cut on the light. I recall me and my mother were the only ones living there at this time. I told her about the dark figure. I had a speaker close to the bed which I kicked so hard I broke it. Knocking the three and a half foot speaker across the room.

Some years later about four or five, I was get loaded with friends. Now before this, I had noticed a change in my countenance. But had not discerned what it was. While tripping I caused all in the car to see altogether, seeing we all thought the same thoughts, at the same time.

I pointed it out and they saw. Suddenly all in the car could not breath, we all at the exact same time opened all four doors and defang to jump out of the car gasping for air. They continued to go to Archie's house and try and explain what happened. Of course everyone said what y'all tripping on. I listened and said nothing, knowing it could not be explained.

A day came after that I could not eat, and this went on a while. Till I became dehydrated to the point I crapped so and was in great pain. I had done never damage and had not eaten right in at least sixty days. So, being safe I should say I fasted forty days. In a period of about sixty days, though, out of that at least forty.

A night came when there was a powerful electrical storm. Powerful clouds moved across the horizon spaced out. Looking like warships with light striking out in five or 6 places at once. I was amazed at the power of these storms. I then dosed off and fell asleep.

While sleeping, I saw, and Angel dressed in a breastplate of light come to me from a bolt of lightning which struck the earth. The Angel walked towards me as if to tell me something, but when I looked at that Angel it was me?

After that I was then I was taunted by spirits, waking me in the night foretelling to me that I would see when opening my eyes. I was heckled by one showing me I could hear people think. Then I saw a UFO oval shape it was amber in color I went up in it.

I came upon an Angel who was pitch black in color, wearing a hood from his clothing. I came upon him so quickly he seemed started and surprised at my coming. He began to pray to me, but when he spoke his mouth did not move, he was a powerful Telepathic. He pointed at a machine and gave me a choice in which way to go.

I left that place quickly and passed to a place where I heard a multitude of men calling me. These men were held in great darkness and a pale green light on the horizon. I walked towards the dark place where those men's voices came from. They announced themselves to me by the thousands then a few spoke.

They were former presidents and great men of the earth. These are those held by that dark Angel, which I fled from and did not pray with him when he prayed. His hand reached out to shake my hand after he prayed, and I did not shake his hand. He became angry with me, and I fled to the place of those men held in darkness.

As they spoke to me, they told me they were all wrong and asked me not to shake this dark angel's hand as they all had done. And I left that place.

After this I recall a gland, or something popped in the back of my head, and I became telepathic. Those on the other side had warned me I had gone too deep and could see even them. When I was awake all things became out of cinque as if I knew ahead of time things, names of people and such.

It was told to me I was like Adam, and from that point forward began my research of things. I found also in the books of Adam. Satan was black, blacker than we of earth. Coming from Jupiter, he was Telepathic, and they are Grigori, his ship is a great light. That is to say, his throne which these ships are called are big lights.

Then there came a day somewhat like other days, when I rested deeply, I heard a man's voice who talked or taught. Then after hearing him in a consistent way for some weeks. I fell into a deep rest in the middle of the day.

I was in a dark place, pitch black in my mind. Suddenly I saw a door opened, it was light on the other side, all the while hearing that man teach. So, I went through the door and was walking in what was like a cloud. I followed the man's voice into the midst, and it got closer.

I came to a place where I saw four or five men who were really white, sitting in a trance looking at a place the man's voice spoke. So, I turned to see what they looked at, and soon as I looked, I went into the trance. And was taught Telepathy in a fast way, given understanding.

I snapped out of the trance and looked and saw those four or five men, maybe four, still in the trance. I looked back at the light that was in the cloud and again was in the trance being taught.

Telepathy.

After this I came out of the trance and saw two men standing to the right of that light in the cloud and those four men sitting still in that trance. Those two men asked me if I could see them? I told them yes; I can see you; they asked me to repeat some things. And explained to me some problems of retention with memory.

They said things like I would not remember, but they put something in me that would come out one day. And people would believe what I said. They told me I did not belong in that place and must leave. I told them I did not want to leave because I liked the Telepathy they taught.

They told me to look at the cloud and pointed behind me. I turned and looked; they asked what did I see? I told them I see my friend Archie and going to the gym to play basketball. They told me I must go, and remember what they taught, and one day they would return. Then I heard the white ones speak, as did we all speak in one voice.

They told me to wake up and remember all they had taught me. Then I awoke and it was in the fall of the year. And I heard leaves which crackled from footsteps that approached the house after a short while, while I contemplated. I heard the knock at the door. I got up and opened it, it was my friend Archie and he asked if I wanted to go to the gym to play basketball.

I responded no and did not and nor had we any immediate plans to go to that gym. I recall he had mentioned it about two weeks prior, since I had been out of state a while. I had recently returned home, so going to the gym was not a practice of mine.

I think the next day I sat on the front porch, while sitting, I thought of two young men I did not know. These two men, I had seen also about two weeks before. And I thought; why did I think of these two young men I did not know? So, I thought, they must be coming down the street like before when I saw them last.

So, I got up to look and could not see up the street because of a hedgerow which ran out to the street from my neighbor's house. So, after standing up I went out to the sidewalk to look up the street and saw clearly those two young men I saw weeks before. And had thought of again, walking down the street toward me.

I guess what I supposed in all this, was it possible something possessed me. Or was a part of me taken from me when that ship came, and then taught me, and put that part back in me in that storm. And caused me to see Satan, the Grigori before I learned these things in the books.

Or how did I know Adam was a Telepathic who fasted, teaching his children. Later that became the teachings of the prophets. These are the things which led me, where I went in my study.

Did I stand in a place with Gods Holy Seven angels? Or was I the seventh Angel, because when I counted those outside that light there were seven or eight. So, it was as if I stood with Michael and his Angels, even before I studied from the books and knew these things. It was as if I knew its all ahead of my learning. Even forty years.

And remember this, I heard the man teach after that one time, but seemed far away. But they all told me one day they would return. Of course, there are other things, I didn't write, but for now.

AFTERWORD

I would say my story came into existence because of those things which came to me. Things talking about Telepathy, and they were mad at me because I did not remember. They taunted me by pointing out Telepathy to me. There was a point I became afraid to sleep, because of those things on the other side. I believe they can join with you, to the point of you being possessed. I won't deny there are bad things there, tactical things. Things like the thing that sat down with me and taught me the game "Nuclear War" that thing a "Dark Shadow" which appeared to me in two or three dreams. This Shadow Thing sat across from me showing me the game. Again, I was at his Grand Palace and White City, and red curtains and carpets, with beautiful Greek type columns throughout the Great City. Nuclear War, I've been building it forty-five years maybe? I've created almost a new technology to play it, it's a revolution. But because of where it comes from and who taught me the game, I am afraid to release it. You know that Dark Shadow knighted me at his Palace, he gave me a sword which killed or destroyed at the distance. It was an elegant sword that had jewels on its sheath. Funny thing is I think years had passed and I was in a place in a dream where I was using this sword given to me years before. Yet I knew nothing of Telepathy, but after I stood with those seven, I saw another dream or likely vision. I was able to see Telepathy, I'm not a mind reader nor do I try and read minds. Its not my capability, but somehow, I seem to know the teaching before or read it. Or I'm looking for stuff I know is in there yet never read it.

CONCLUSION

10 And one of us He commanded that we should teach Noah all their medicines; for He knew that they would not walk in uprightness, nor strive in righteousness.

11 And we did according to all His words: all the malignant evil ones we bound in the place of condemnation, and a tenth part of them we left that they might be subject before Satan on the earth.

12 And we explained to Noah all the medicines of their diseases, together with their seductions, how he might heal them with herbs of the earth. 13. And Noah wrote down all things in a book as we instructed him concerning every kind of medicine. Thus, the evil spirits were precluded from (hurting) the sons of Noah.

14 And he gave all that he had written to Shem, his eldest son; for he loved him exceedingly above all his sons.

Tobit 3

17 And Raphael was sent to heal them both, that is, to scale away the whiteness of Tobit's eyes, and to give Sara the daughter of Raguel for a wife to Tobias the son of Tobit; and to bind Asmodeus the evil spirit.

Tobit 6

4 To whom the angel said, Open the fish, and take the heart and the liver and the gall, and put them up safely.

Tobit 6

8 As for the gall, it is good to anoint a man that hath whiteness in his eyes, and he shall be healed.

CHRIST WILL RETURN THE SAME DAY HE LEFT

Because time has been stuck together, it will be the same day he left we see him, coming.

Esdras 13:32

32 And the time shall be when these things shall come to pass, and the signs shall happen which I shewed thee before, and then shall my Son be declared, whom thou sawest as a man ascending.

"(Now that he ascended, what is it but that he also descended first into the lower parts of the earth? He that descended is the same also that ascended up far above all heavens, that he might fill all things.)"
Ephesians 4:9-10 KJV

Note because of zero time, Christ can leave and come back the same day and time yet have thousands of years pass. Why, because time has failed its not an accurate measure after this point and time.

"And when he had spoken these things, while they beheld, he was taken up; and a cloud received him out of their sight. And while they looked steadfastly toward heaven as he went up, behold, two men stood by them in white apparel; which also said, Ye men of Galilee, why stand ye gazing up into heaven? this same Jesus, which is taken up from you into heaven, shall so come in like manner as ye have seen him go into heaven."
Acts 1:9-11 KJV

In like manner means you are seeing something which won't happen for about 2500 years and when you see him again it's like the same day he left, because it is.

"So, Christ was once offered to bear the sins of many; and unto them that look for him shall he appear the second time without sin unto salvation."
Hebrews 9:28 KJV

CHRIST WAS NOT RECOGNIZE WHEN RESURRECTED WHY?

"After that he appeared in another form unto two of them, as they walked, and went into the country."
Mark 16:12 KJV

form
/fôrm/
See definition
1. the visible shape or configuration of something.

"But when the morning was now come, Jesus stood on the shore: but the disciples knew not that it was Jesus. This is now the third time that Jesus shewed himself to his disciples, after that he was risen from the dead."
John 21:4, 14 KJV

And Jesus answered and said, while he taught in the temple, how say the scribes that Christ is the son of David? For David himself said by the Holy Ghost, The LORD said to my Lord, sit thou on my right hand, Till I make thine enemies thy footstool. David therefore himself calleth him Lord; and whence is he then his son? And the common people heard him gladly.
Mark 12:35-37 KJV

IS THIS CHILD CHRIST?

"And it came to pass on the seventh day, that the child died. And the servants of David feared to tell him that the child was dead: for they said, Behold, while the child was yet alive, we spake unto him, and he would not hearken unto our voice: how will he then vex himself, if we tell him that the child is dead?"
2 Samuel 12:18 KJV

IF SO, WOULD HE BE HALF BLACK?

"And he that sat was to look upon like a jasper and a sardine stone: and there was a rainbow round about the throne, in sight like unto an emerald."
Revelation 4:3 KJV

"I am black, but comely, O ye daughters of Jerusalem, As the tents of Kedar, As the curtains of Solomon."
Song of Solomon 1:5 KJV

This child I believe to be Christ.

33 And when all the people hear his voice, every man shall in their own land leave the battle they have one against another.
34 And an innumerable multitude shall be gathered together, as thou sawest them, willing to come, and to overcome him by fighting.
35 But he shall stand upon the top of the mount Sion.

"Jesus saith unto her, Woman, why weepest thou? whom seekest thou? She, supposing him to be the gardener, saith unto him, Sir, if thou have borne him, hence, tell me where thou hast laid him, and I will take him away. Jesus saith unto her, touch me not; for I am not yet ascended to my Father: but go to my brethren, and say unto them, I ascend unto my Father, and your Father; and to my God, and your God."
John 20:15, 17 KJV

AND FOR THOSE AGAINST MEDICINE AND DRUGS NO EVIDENCE FOR THOSE AGAINST MEDICINE WHEN ITS NOT WRITTEN TO BE AGAINST IT.

10 And one of us He commanded that we should teach Noah all their medicines; for He knew that they would not walk in uprightness, nor strive in righteousness.

11 And we did according to all His words: all the malignant evil ones we bound in the place of condemnation, and a tenth part of them we left that they might be subject before Satan on the earth.

12 And we explained to Noah all the medicines of their diseases, together with their seductions, how he might heal them with herbs of the earth. 13. And Noah wrote down all things in a book as we instructed him concerning every kind of medicine. Thus the evilspirits were precluded from (hurting) the sons of Noah.

14 And he gave all that he had written to Shem, his eldest son; for he loved him exceedingly above all his sons.

1- Esdras 7

53 And that there should be shewed a paradise, whose fruit endureth forever, wherein is security and medicine, since we shall not enter into it?

Enoch

Chapter 28

1 Then I went to another place from the desert, towards the east of that mountain which I had approached.

2 There I beheld choice trees, particularly those which produce the sweet-smelling drugs, frankincense and myrrh; and trees unlike to each other.

Tobit 3

17 And Raphael was sent to heal them both, that is, to scale away the whiteness of Tobit's eyes, and to give Sara the daughter of Raguel for a wife to Tobias the son of Tobit; and to bind Asmodeus the evil spirit.

Tobit 6

4 To whom the angel said, Open the fish, and take the heart and the liver and the gall, and put them up safely.

Tobit 6

8 As for the gall, it is good to anoint a man that hath whiteness in his eyes, and he shall be healed. What is the dimensions of Time?

Times: extent is what is past, what is now, what is to come.

- which extents could be forever

Zero Time:

If there is motion there without time?

If motion without time is possible how much more can be accomplished in a single point in time.

Fact is: I believe UFO's could interact with us and we not see them simply existing in the same space but at different times, like how we live in a place day to day, yet at different times.

No time calculation, not occupying space and time.

Example: if you get up and move out of a chair.

I as a time traveler, I come sit in your chair two minutes after you get up.

1- I would have to enter your room a zero time so as to not affect the time you are in. (A) If I could alter all time, and I jump back in Time all time would adjust and go back to the day I went to. But to disrupt this effect you enter with zero time. Co-existing with Time, without disrupting time must be a possibility if time travel exist.

Solution = to zero time can inter time and not alter actual time or linear time.

di·men·sion

/dəˈmen(t)SH(ə)n/

noun

plural noun: dimensions

1. a measurable extent of some kind, such as length, breadth, depth, or height.

Amen.

APPENDIX OR ADDENDUM

(Reference)

UFO Coverup Live 1988

UFO Cover-Up Live 1988 – 1989

Anonymous (Condor)**Richard Doty** (Falcon)**Robert Emenegger** (Self)**Mike Farrell** (Self)**Les Marshak**

[UFO Cover Up Live ⏵ Project Blue Book Alien Proof Mike Farrell Interviews ⏵ 1988 TV Documentary](youtu.be)

YouTube Temple Mount 2011 Dome of the Rock

https://youtu.be/JIoHE6P8gOk

CHRONOLOGY

I guess my story started in the 1960's when I prayed to God to teach me Telepathy, and so me a ship, and I also talked to his angels about this. In the 1970's. The ship that appears in Winnipeg, Manitoba in about 1971 flashing red, white, and disappearing then jumped with the double flash was the same ship I saw landed. Red whit and disappearing is a unique identifier, or signature.

Temple Mount and The Dome of the Rock in 2011 is the second ship to do the double flash. The double flash appears to be communications which can be traced back thousands of years to be able to decipher.

GLOSSARY

Definitions of words based on two or three. Which is the basis of Christian teachings judgment is based on two or three apostles, prophets, or witnesses to events, it is a requirement for being taught. Its law, you are just by two or three not endless what if this or that's.

AEON:

5 When all creation visible and invisible, as the Lord created it, shall end, then every man goes to the great judgement, and then all-time shall perish, and the years, and thenceforward there will be neither months nor days nor hours, they will be stuck together and will not be counted.

6 There will be one Aeon, and all the righteous who shall escape the Lord's great judgement, shall be collected in the great Aeon, for the righteous the great Aeon will begin, and they will live eternally, and then too there will be amongst them neither labor, nor sickness, nor humiliation, nor anxiety, nor need, nor violence, nor night, nor darkness, but. great light.

THE GOSPEL ACCORDING TO MARY MAGDALENE

23) In a Aeon I was released from a world, and in a Type from a type, and from the fetter of oblivion which is transient.

24) From this time on will I attain to the rest of the time, of the season, of the Aeon, in silence.

ZERO-TIME as it relates to the Aeon, it's a place of zero time and capabilities from the spiritual to the physical.

Gnostic Scriptures and Fragments

EIGHTH DAY

Barnabas 13

I shall begin the eighth day, that is, the beginning of the other world.

10 For which cause we observe the eighth day with gladness, in which Jesus rose from the dead; and having manifested himself to his disciples, ascended into heaven.

Secrets of Enoch 33

AND I appointed the eighth day also, that the eighth day should be the first-created after my work, and that the first seven revolve in the form of the seventh thousand, and that at the beginning of the eighth thousand there should be a time of not-counting, endless, with neither years nor months nor weeks nor days nor hours.

Resurrection and Time Travel, period of 1000 to cleanse the earth to some degree.

FLOOD - caused by time being stuck together by bringing water from the six other periods of time. This causes. Less water to be in one period of a thousand years. That might cause droughts in other periods of time terraforming literally.

Time Travel

The eight day is the division of each millennium, atmosphere divided by thousand-year increments. Each having its own allotment of atmospheric elements.

FORM OF THAT STAR

1st Book of Infancy

3 And at the same time there appeared to them an angel in the form of that star which had before been their guide in their journey; the light of which they followed till they returned into their own country.

Enoch 85

2. And behold a single star fell from heaven.

4. (Partial) and surveyed heaven; when behold I saw many stars which descended, and projected themselves from heaven to where the first star was,

de·scend

/dəˈsend/

See definitions in:

All

Biology

Music

verb

1. move or fall downward.

Projected

8. make a projection of (the earth, sky, etc.) on a plane surface.

Jasher 8

10 And when thy servants went out from the house of Terah, to go to our respective homes to abide there for the night, we lifted our eyes to heaven, and we saw a great star coming from the east, and the same star ran with great speed, and swallowed up four great stars, from the four sides of the heavens.

11 And thy servants were astonished at the sight which we saw, and were greatly terrified, and we made our judgment upon the sight, and knew by our wisdom the proper interpretation thereof, that this thing applies to the child that is born to Terah, who will grow up and multiply greatly, and become powerful, and kill all the kings of the earth, and inherit all their lands, he and his seed forever.

FOUR WINDS OF THE EARTH / WHIRLWINDS / SEVEN THUNDERS

Definition, a product of Time Stuck Together, UFOs, in Whirlwinds. Storms so strong they can destroy the earth.

"And I saw another angel ascending from the east, having the seal of the living God: and he cried with a loud voice to the four angels, to whom it was given to hurt the earth and the sea,"
Revelation 7:2 KJV

Esdras 15

34 Behold clouds from the east and from the north unto the south, and they are very horrible to look upon, full of wrath and storm.

35 They shall smite one upon another, and they shall smite down a great multitude of stars upon the earth, even their own star; and blood shall be from the sword unto the belly,

39 And strong winds shall arise from the east and shall open it; and the cloud which he raised up in wrath, and the star stirred to cause fear toward the east and west wind, shall be destroyed.

40 The great and mighty clouds shall be puffed up full of wrath, and the star, that they may make all the earth afraid, and them that dwell therein; and they shall pour out over every high and eminent place an horrible star,

"And I looked, and behold, a whirlwind came out of the north, a great cloud, and a fire infolding itself, and a brightness was about it, and out of the midst thereof as the colour of amber, out of the midst of the fire."
Ezekiel 1:4 KJV

In the Spirit of the lord, is Telepathy, so then through the study of Telepathy, you gain understanding of the Lord.

GREAT LIGHT

Great Light
9 And in the night in which the Lord's day was drawing on, as the soldiers kept guard two by two in a watch, there was a great voice in the heaven; and they saw the heavens opened, and two men descend from thence with great light and approach the tomb. And that stone which was put at the door rolled of itself and made way in part; and the tomb was opened, and both the young men entered in.

great
/grāt/
adjective
1.of an extent, amount, or intensity considerably above the normal or average.

1st Book of Adam and Eve

2 He began with transforming his hosts; in his hands was a flashing fire, and they were in a great light.

Note possible meaning of big light.

"And it came to pass, that, as I made my journey, and was come nigh unto Damascus about noon, suddenly there shone from heaven a great light round about me."
Acts 22:6 KJV

HEAVEN DEFINED AS

Example: "And God said, let there be lights in the firmament of the heaven to divide the day from the night; and let them be for signs, and for seasons, and for days, and years: and let them be for lights in the firmament of the heaven to give light upon the earth: and it was so. And God made two great lights; the greater light to rule the day, and the lesser light to rule the night: he made the stars also."
Genesis 1:14-16 KJV

Heaven is described as, all these things, so Pillar of Fire reach all that.

fir·ma·ment
/ˈfərməmənt/
nounLITERARY
the heavens or the sky, especially when regarded as a tangible thing.

But Note: it's also including everything that has time stuck together, and the means of it being joined as one. So, no division remains among the host. Access to, whole.

Question remains: that zero time is a part of Heaven - exist without time, step back and forth in time or forward in (Time: to prepare a place) for you says deductive reasoning, that's going into the future.

What is reach Heaven capabilities?

HOLY GHOST

It's my belief there is an entity or entities which are capable of using our body as host. This entity seems to join together as I am a witness.

"But the Comforter, which is the Holy Ghost, whom the Father will send in my name, he shall teach you all things, and bring all things to your remembrance, whatsoever I have said unto you."
John 14:26 KJV

"But ye shall receive power, after that the Holy Ghost is come upon you: and ye shall be witnesses unto me both in Jerusalem, and in all Judæa, and in Samaria, and unto the uttermost part of the earth."
Acts 1:8 KJV

PILLAR OF FIRE

Jasher 23 examples 42 And a pillar of fire appeared to him that reached from the earth to heaven, and a cloud of glory upon the mountain, and the glory of the Lord was seen in the cloud.
1-defined as reach from earth to Heaven:

"And mount Sinai was altogether on a smoke, because the LORD descended upon it in fire: and the smoke thereof ascended as the smoke of a furnace, and the whole mount quaked greatly."
Exodus 19:18 KJV

So, the pillar of fire has light that come off it it can consume things, winds which part seas and left ice and snow in strange places, capable of Time travel and building worlds.

THRONE

The Book of Enoch 14
17 Attentively I surveyed it, and saw that it contained an exalted throne;

18 The appearance of which was like that of frost; while its circumference resembled the orb of the brilliant sun; and there was the voice of the cherubim.

cir·cum·fer·ence
/sərˈkəmf(ə)rəns/
noun
the enclosing boundary of a curved geometric figure, especially a circle.

great
/grāt/
adjective
1. of an extent, amount, or intensity considerably above the normal or average.
"the article was of great interest"
2. of ability, quality, or eminence considerably above the normal or average.

1st Book of Adam and Eve 27
2 He began with transforming his hosts; in his hands was a flashing fire, and they were in a great light.
3 He then placed his throne near the mouth of the cave because he could not enter it by reason of their prayers. And he shed light into the cave, until the cave glistened over Adam and Eve, while his hosts began to sing praises.

SEVENFOLD DOCTRINE OF THE WHOLE CREATION
The sevenfold doctrine is written once as I can determine. But requires a second Prophet to be established. All I can add if I am a Prophet of God is this.
-it appears to be a terraforming process, which equally divides the atmosphere and all it component's parts. All things time itself is divided by seven and combined in place to move elements from one period of time to another. While sticking time together to move it place to place back and forward in time.

Sticking time together to raise the dead, possibly cause catastrophic events to repeat themselves, things like meteorites which hit us long ago would hit us again.

Enoch 92

12 Afterwards, in the seventh week, a perverse generation shall arise; abundant shall be its deeds, and all its deeds perverse. During its completion, the righteous shall be selected from the everlasting plant of righteousness; and to them shall be given the sevenfold doctrine of his whole creation.

SEVEN STARS

So, by this description the seven stars where here before heaven. Or the fallen angels have been cast back in Time on Earth before heaven was created.

Secrets of Enoch 27

I showed each one of them its road, and the seven stars each one of them in its heaven, that they go thus, and I saw that it was good.

Secrets of Enoch 30

4 On the first uppermost circle I placed the stars, Kruno, and on the second Aphrodite, on the third Aris, on the fifth Zeus, on the sixth Ermis, on the seventh lesser the moon, and adorned it with the lesser stars.

5 And on the lower I placed the sun for the illumination of day, and the moon and stars for the illumination of night.

6 The sun that it should go according to each animal (sc. signs of the zodiac), twelve, and I appointed the succession of the months and their names and lives, their thundering's, and their hour-markings, how they should succeed.

Enoch 21

1 Then I made a circuit to a place in which nothing was completed.

2 And there I beheld neither the tremendous workmanship of an exalted heaven, nor of an established earth, but a desolate spot, prepared, and terrific.

3 There, too, I beheld seven stars of heaven bound in it together,

SEVEN THUNDERS

Though not defined it can be observed by two books specifically, definition sealed it can be deduced from two or three.

Esdras 15:34

Behold clouds from the east and from the north unto the south, and they are very horrible to look upon, full of wrath and storm.

38 And then shall there come great storms from the south, and from the north, and another part from the west.

39 And strong winds shall arise from the east, and shall open it; and the cloud which he raised up in wrath, and the star stirred to cause fear toward the east and west wind, shall be destroyed.

40 The great and mighty clouds shall be puffed up full of wrath, and the star, that they may make all the earth afraid, and them that dwell therein; and they shall pour out over every high and eminent place an horrible star,

"Thus, saith the LORD of hosts, Behold, evil shall go forth from nation to nation, and a great whirlwind shall be raised up from the coasts of the earth."

Jeremiah 25:32 KJV

"Behold, a whirlwind of the LORD is gone forth in fury, even a grievous whirlwind: it shall fall grievously upon the head of the wicked."

Jeremiah 23:19 KJV

"And after these things I saw four angels standing on the four corners of the earth, holding the four winds of the earth, that the wind should not blow on the earth, nor on the sea, nor on any tree."

Revelation 7:1 KJV

STAR, multiple definitions

But parts of the meaning of stars is other worlds which fall to earth, as well as ships which look like stars.

and the stars of heaven fell unto the earth, even as a fig tree casteth her untimely figs, when she is shaken of a mighty wind."

Revelation 6:13 KJV

Enoch 87

1 Then I looked at that one of the four white men, who came forth first.

2 He seized the first star which fell down from heaven.

3 And, binding it hand and foot, he cast it into a valley; a valley narrow, deep, stupendous, and gloomy.

This depicts stars which fell to earth at different period of time.

NOTE: no definition of how long is the period of them falling, hundreds, thousands or millions of years?

Enoch 18

16 The stars which roll over fire are those which transgressed the commandment of God before their time arrived; for they came not in their proper season. Therefore, was He offended with them, and bound them, until the period of the consummation of their crimes in the secret year.

TIME TRAVEL

365 days times 1000 years = 365, 000 days.

This is a grid interlaid, so to have days within days so each day is interlaid with 365 other days in one location or coordinate which repeats itself day to day.

Based on a theory that there's a place with zero time. And probably, someone solved the solution from "Zero Time" From the further there is one which claims to achieved find and escape from the place of no Time.

365,000 x 7 = 2,555,000 days or 7000 years. It appears tied into another more larger grid, for universal travel.

2,555,000 divided by 2,555,001 years equals

0.999999608610721 Years so this stuck time together Time Barrier Broken is the concept of resurrection and other. Time Stuck together puts everyone ever born in the here and now.

here and now
/ˌhir ən ˈnou/
phrase of here
at this very moment; at the present time.

Though it appears, they come forward at different rates, from the dead to the living.
Tracking Michael Proves Time Travel.

CHRIST FIRSTBORN, in the 8th millennium Time Stuck together causing Christ to be raised in the 5th millennium.
Christ the First fruit, was raised in the eighth day, in about 480 years or so.

Barnabas 13
I shall begin the eighth day, that is, the beginning of the other world.
10 For which cause we observe the eighth day with gladness, in which Jesus rose from the dead; and having manifested himself to his disciples, ascended into heaven.
Michael shows up at the first resurrection with Christ yet he's not resurrected and possibly not yet born. As with other of the Archangels

8th Day in less than 500 years

"And at that time shall Michael stand up, the great prince which standeth for the children of thy people: and there shall be a time of trouble, such as never was since there was a nation even to that same time: and at that time thy people shall be delivered, every one that shall be found written in the book."
Daniel 12:1 KJV

The seven white ones sent back to the war in heaven from the resurrection and judgment a consideration Time in the future.

Enoch 31
5 Then God commanded the three angels, Michael, Gabriel and Raphael, each to bring what he had brought, and give it to Adam. And they did so, one by one.

Michael tells Enoch they are his ancestors.

Enoch 58
9 His name was Dendayen in the east of the garden, where the elect and the righteous will dwell; where he received it from my ancestor, who was man, from Adam the first of men, whom the Lord of spirits made.

Nicodemus 21
4 The archangel Michael farther commanded us to go beyond Jordan, to an excellent and fat country, where there are many who rose from the dead along with us for the proof of the resurrection of Christ.

Deductive Reasoning proves Moses and Elias are traveling back in Time having come before the resurrection. Time Travel being shown us.

"And behold, there appeared unto them Moses and Elias talking with him."
Matthew 17:3 KJV

TIME STUCK TOGETHER

TIME
Time was defined as fixed, as in today, question when Time is fixed, or was there a period before being fixed where Time Was Stuck together. Time appears fixed here on earth at 7 periods of thousand-year increments separated from the other thousand year periods.

"But, beloved, be not ignorant of this one thing, that one day is with the Lord as a thousand years, and a thousand years as one day."
2 Peter 3:8 KJV

These are literally thousand years periods on some calculation which is dividing all things by seven, sun light, wind, atmospheric clouds,

TWELVE (12) STARS
"And there appeared a great wonder in heaven; a woman clothed with the sun, and the moon under her feet, and upon her head a crown of twelve stars:"
Revelation 12:1 KJV

4 On the first uppermost circle I placed the stars, Kruno, and on the second Aphrodit, on the third Aris, on the fifth Zeus, on the sixth Ermis, on the seventh lesser the moon, and adorned it with the lesser stars.
5 And on the lower I placed the sun for the illumination of day, and the moon and stars for the illumination of night.
6 The sun that it should go according to each animal (sc. signs of the zodiac), twelve, and I appointed the succession of the months and their names and lives, their thunderings, and their hour-markings, how they should succeed.
7 Then evening came and morning came the fifth day.

WAR IN HEAVEN

Time Travel

This event happens maybe in 1500 years, it hasn't happened yet but has. It happens in the 8th or 9th millennium, and we are in the seventh.

Time Travel Michael and His angels sent from the future to back in time.

Enoch 89

29 And I saw a throne erected in a delectable land.

30 Upon this sat the Lord of the sheep, who received all the sealed books.

31 Which were open before him.

32 Then the Lord called the first seven white ones, and commanded them to bring before him the first of the first stars, which preceded the stars whose form partly resembled that of horses; the first star, which fell down first;

"And there was war in heaven: Michael and his angels fought against the dragon; and the dragon fought and his angels and prevailed not; neither was their place found any more in heaven."
Revelation 12:7-8 KJV

Michael and his angels are sent back in time to seize, angels from other worlds which are come down before they should have.

BIBLIOGRAPHY

1st and 2nd Books of Adam and Eve, Esdras, Levi, Tobit, Hermes, Daniel, Revelation, Index Apocrypha, Missing Books of The Bible King James The Book of Enoch and the Secrets of Enoch

How long did the light of the Big Bang last?
To submit Ask Astro questions, please email askastro@astronomy.com
For columnist queries, please contact astronomyeditorial@astronomy.com

How long was there darkness before the Big Bang?
New Science Weekly Magazine
For all other enquiries, please email customerhelp@newscientist.com

In The Big Bang Cosmology
Earth sky.org

What particles existed after the Big Bang?

- Email: visits.service@cern.ch

CERN
Esplanade des Particules 1
P.O. Box
1211 Geneva 23
Switzerland

American Museum of Natural History
Formation of the solar system
200 Central Park West

New York, NY 10024-5102

Phone: 212-769-5100

Was the Sun formed 4.5 billion years ago?

NASA Solar System

Solarsystem.NASA.gov

Astronomy

The fog didn't lift until 1 billion years after the Big Bang

To submit Ask Astro questions, please email askastro@astronomy.com

For columnist queries, please contact astronomyeditorial@astronomy.com

How long did it take for the sun to become visible

After between three and ten million years, the young Sun's solar wind would have cleared.

lvpKRJinMW4cxLMPsDAJjSCaG8cPmnAAAAAElFTkSuQmCChttps://en.m.wikipedia.org ›
wiki

How long before plant life began to form?

Plant Life

Brewery House 36 Milford Street Salisbury Wiltshire SP1 2AP England United Kingdom

Tel: 01722 342730

Email: enquiries@plantlife.org.uk

How the Earth and moon formed? explained

University of Chicago

Office of Communications

5801 S. Ellis Ave., Suite 120, Chicago, IL 60637

(773) 702-8360

news@uchicago.edu

Zodiac Image to define the location of the "War In Heaven"

Page Updated 03/02/2022

Copyright © 2023 | Western Washington University | Accessibility

http://archimedespalimpsest.org/about/

http://archimedespalimpsest.org/about/

The Archimedes Palimpsest Project is managed by Michael B. Toth. Mike is the President and CTO of R.B.Toth Associates

The Archimedean spiral is a spiral named after the 3rd-century BC Greek mathematician Archimedes. It is the locus corresponding to the locations over time of a point moving away from a fixed point with a constant speed along a line that rotates with constant angular velocity. Wikipedia

DJF/JOC/EFR
Copyright information
Accessibility statement
School of Mathematics and Statistics
University of St Andrews, Scotland

Taking the pole as the centre of inversion, the spiral of Archimedes $r = a\theta$ inverts to the hyperbolic spiral $r = a/\theta$.

AUTOBIOGRAPHY

I suppose I should start at the beginning, when as a child, I don't know ten or so. After me and my brother and cousin had saw an article about possible UFOs in the Bible.

This had interested me more than anything else at that time about God being raised in the church. I prayed sincerely to God and his angels. Asking them to teach me Telepathy and show me a ship. I guess I did this for some nights.

After some years, my mother and two sisters came home from church one weekday. As we hurried into the house to try and catch StarTrek which at the time was a series. Now StarTrek played until 1969, so, the UFO filmed over Winnipeg, Manitoba I am not sure of the year.

Well, why is that important? It could determine the year we saw the ship landed on Joseph Weller School across from the house. Why that ship, I believe when it aired the ship changed colors from red to white and blinking out as it flew. The current film does not show color changing.

So, my sister then spoke out and said look at the big red light on the school. We all looked for a while unsure of what it was. They all continued in the house, but i continued to watch. I took a seat on the porch.

The light after a couple of minutes turns from red to white. I ran into the house and told my sisters and mom. Irene came and looked I think the others remained uninterested. Irene went back into the house. The ship then appeared to vanish, I ran into the house and announced that.

Maybe a sister came and left back into the house. I continued to sit as if I knew it was still there. It reappeared red, and white and vanished, staying in each cycle of light a couple of minutes. This went on close to a half hour.

I recall after that I became very tired. So tired I went into the house and straight to bed, falling into a deep sleep. After that, I always seemed to be unsure what the thing was I never saw fly.
Well, what can I say, my life has been interesting and somewhat backwards. What I mean by that is I accomplished a lot, but normally got cut down before I could blossom. I was born in San Jose California in 1955. My family had just relocated from the central valley to the city. My earliest recollections as a child go back until I was about two and half years old, I can soundly say.

So, I talked to some of my cousins' brothers and sister who were all older about and event with my grandmother. The event was roasting hot dogs on a stick in the country over a open fire. It was a warm night and the fourth of July. That's not so significant, but I was called over and my mother was trying to introduce me to her mother.

The thing is I was three when she died about six or seven months later, I was still two few months from being three. So, at that age I had pretty good comprehension and my older cousin s have said they remembered that day after I brought it to their recollection. And if we go back to her mother who was Indian and spoke Cherokee.

But to my recollection they said we were creek Indians. But her story was strange, her parents died when she was about twelve. We believe she was born in Mexico. Its pretty hard to track but her mother was Sally Shields, and they are the Buffalo Soldiers. I know we had a relative from England who lived in Australia came to America and owned slaves.

Now the Seminole Chief Wildcat after he was captured in Florida, was in the Trail of Tears and went into Oklahoma. Wildcat left Oklahoma and they went down in Mexico Piedras Negras on the border. They also got land from the Mexican Government for fighting Apache's who would com into Mexico. Thing is many slaves Kickapoo Indians others went with them into Mexico.

Also, about the time the civil war was starting. The slave owner sold his plantation, he had black children who tried to pass for white. Some got caught and fined $500.00 in Texas trying to pass for white. So, by the time the civil war started I think they were down in Mexico as well. I had always heard I had a great, great, grandfather, who was a chief.

My, great grandmother father was his son. He was told, never to come back when they left, but to my knowledge it was in Mexico where she orphaned. It believed they died of the consumption and probably why they were told never to come back. Because of those European sicknesses. After while I was thinking in those days it was better to be anything but black.

I guess the reason I mention these people who passed for white or tried to. Was my great-grandmother saying she used to live with some white people and we believe that may be the family. But in fact, these are both white and black, but she ran away nor tried to at least number of times. The she married into a family who I believe are Norwegian and the children were part black. And there is a black part of this family, as well as a white part of this family. With the coat of arms as well. It appears they came from Germany, but I haven't tracked them. Our DNA shows we are Norwegian, Switzerland and from that region, Norse.

So, we heard stories about my great, great or great grandfather wearing to guns in Texas, and had a lot of people scared of him. And it was he I think they said who wanted the squaw which was my great grandfather, who I believe to her from another man who may have been black. Well, I think the Norwegian was half black as well.

But the fact is my grandfather was I think born on the Oklahoma reservation. This is from where my family names come from my grandfather. He was an outlaw that to use was hidden. Oh, we heard stories about him. Starting about age twelve I think he may have killed a man. Married young and had fifteen children from his wife. And DNA test are showing us perhaps others.

Well during the twenties, I think he was running boot leg liquor on the east coast, in the south and up north in Chicago probably. He had been shot twice, once with a shotgun who the doctor says should have killed a mule at that distance. And the other a pistol, well, that one he would tell us how. I figured it was because he was committing a crime somehow. He had about five or six cuts on each hand from grabbing a knife with someone trying to kill him. And he was cutting buckshot out until the day he died, twelve gage shot I believe.

They say he was paid ninety-three thousand from John Dillinger I can't say. We used to think it was simply rumor but many sworn by it. It was more li was baby Face Nelson who he worked with. Maybe they were organized enough to pull of crime in many states yet funnel the money to one location. I do see Baby Face Nelson working in Oklahoma Bank robberies and that's probably where they found my grandfather, if they did.

It was all hear say until we found both my grandfather and grandmother working in the First National Bank in Oklahoma as custodians. And with my grandfather's background I don't think a job in the First National Bank was wise. So, it kind of put a little more meat in that story. The year he worked in the Bank or Banks was 1932, pretty good timing for him to meet the bad guys of the Dillinger Gang and pull a job?

In any case most of my life I never really heard those stories he was just my grandpa. Now he was gone along time form the family. Just before he died, he came back to California, so before his death we had heard some rumors of his exploits we talked, to him asking him directly stuff. Which he never answered and took to his story to the grave.

Let me also mention he was wanted dead or alive in Texas and refused to even drive through Texas all his Life. He had reached the eighties in age. Talked about the black cowboys and new Sara James. I believe that's what her name was who said she was Frank James's daughter and had some tales about Jesse not dying until the nineteen twenties and Frank in the nineteen forties. But like them my grandfather changed his name. When social security came into existence, he told them his name was John Harris. Saying I was born in the house in the country and never had a birth certificate.

He sorts of became a farmer after that, he worked as a Forman for a Japanese man. During the war his boss got interned in the internment camps. But before that rather than loose is property to the government. He sold it to my grandfather for a cheap price, and my grandfather farmed the rest of his life. And became the man I know. He grew cotton had farmworkers and cabin on his property.
It was this particular property in the San Juaquin Valley in which Sara James said she remember that tree which covered his whole house. I'm not sure what kind of a tree it was, but she was one

hundred years old. And said she saw it planted as a child, so to me that was interesting. Whether the stories she told about Frank and Jessy were true I can't say. My grandparents came from a little money. Oil was found on their lands, but they kind of were in hiding so much of the inheritances are lost.

Speaking of which some land we had with oil on it was stolen from my great grandfather. My grandmother was heiress to some oil writes after that. Well, my great grandfather was the son of a white man named John the Baptist Briggs. He had land and lots of it, they in fact were related to the fourth President of the United States James Madison who is my cousin seven times removed. My grandmother Rosella Harris (Willis/Briggs) is listed as royalty on ancestry.

Well, my great grandfather didn't like his father, and felt his father raped his mother. So, he changed his name from Briggs to Willis. But it his grandfather who was more closely related to the President. But John the Baptist Briggs did give him land and wanted to treat him like a son. Much like my grandfather there was a lot of hate in those days. Today I think we still have some mineral rights on the land, but its old money from the eighteen hundreds.

Going back to my childhood, started school at the age of four. I wasn't very happy to start, in the beginning I seemed to have a lot of interest classes. But I think at a early age I became bored with it. Up through high school most teachers felt I never applied myself. Probably true, if you asked me what I wanted to be in those days, I couldn't tell you. I was good at art somewhat, but I didn't think my abilities was natural, at least in drawing. I tried music, but really at that time I couldn't get into it.

I was raised in a track family my father went to state in the long jump. I was a jumper hurdler, ran relay sprints, high jumped a while. Triple Jumped, ranked high in the nation as a junior. Set a high hurdle record for the league. I was injured trying to get to state. But in college I was still 18 years old so did qualify for the junior nationals. Though due to the arrest, which pretty much destroyed my hopes for the Olympics, or any other dream that happened.

I had an injury in the military, which prevented me from ever running track again. I went back to school. Where I really started to apply myself better, but the school failed and destroyed me further. As I had a forgery put on me, and was singled out for a crime, so making it hard to be a part of a class action. Though evidence shows the crimes, power that be just wanted money not caring about the student.

In college driving down after just winning the Golden Gate Conference in track and field. Me and some of my teammate picked up a police tail. One of my track teammates had about an ounce of weed on him.

The police hit us with the light and siren, and I told my teammate to throw out the weed. So, I drove slow for a long way as he threw it out. I then stopped and we were immediately arrested. They walked up and down the road looking for weed but found none.

We were all arrested, the police gave us a rough ride. Hitting chuckholes, bouncing us around. Hitting our heads on the roof threatening to beat us if we kept moving around.

Now when arrested I asked the police to lock my cuffs so they wouldn't get tighter every time I moved. My teammates did not, so by the time we got to jail, their wrist began to get cut.

During the night my couch came and bailed them out and left me in there. Seems the police had fabricated charges of cocaine and green material mixed in it.

Now, I had been busted once before with four joints. Headed to a party with my girlfriend and a friend. The couch bailed me out that time. But of course, I was innocent this time. Sure why would I want to go to jail being convicted for weed not mine. Sure, I told him to throw it out to protect myself. I had just qualified for the Junior Nationals in the long jump.

I missed the state meet, I was held for baking soda, which I used to neutralize battery acid. In those days we had to put water in the batteries. So, handling batteries we carried baking soda.

Missed my finals at school, now this baking soda had probably been in my car over a year or two. Probably when I was bust for the four joints some time before that.

So, in this case it ruins my life, so I no longer had a reason to continue school. And about a few days before almost broke the Junior National Record in the long jump at the West Coast Relays. But scratched on the board about a half inch.

Well, I ended up on probation for the four joints but wanted to go into the army, in an earlier incident. He'd to a party, pulled over and search I couldn't until 2 years they cleaned up the misdemeanor charges later, with probation.

The point is, we have people who are allowed to imagine things or lie against you. They can victimize you, with falsehoods and say they are right. Now for reasons like this, Telepathy should be taught, as a recourse against those who think it's a right to mislead others. That consequence should be I place to punish those who punish others in this way. Fact is there are those out there we should change our ways. Satan had a world; his world is led to the war in heaven. They are fallen; but are we any different than Satan and his world Zeus, by our world earth? How do we have peace with who all need and want the same things, each wanting more than we give the other person as if better.

www.ingramcontent.com/pod-product-compliance
Lightning Source LLC
Chambersburg PA
CBHW061141010526
44118CB00026B/2833